D1299534

TRADITIONAL
COUNTRY
CRAFTS

TRADITIONAL
COUNTRY
CRAFTS

Victoria Dutton

LP LONGMEADOW PRESS

For Victoria and Ferdinand

Copyright © 1996 Todtri Productions Limited. All rights reserved. No part of this
publication may be reproduced, stored in a retrieval system, transmitted, or used in any
form or by any means, electronic, mechanical, photocopying, recording or otherwise
without the prior permission of the copyright holder.

This 1996 edition published by Longmeadow Press
201 High Ridge Road, Stamford, CT 06904.

This book was designed and produced by
Todtri Productions Limited
P.O. Box 572
New York, NY 10116-0572
Fax (212-279-1241)

Printed and bound in Singapore

ISBN 0-681-10470-8

Publisher: Robert M. Tod
Designer and Art Director: Ron Pickless
Editor: Nicolas Wright
Typeset and DTP: Blanc Verso/UK

CONTENTS

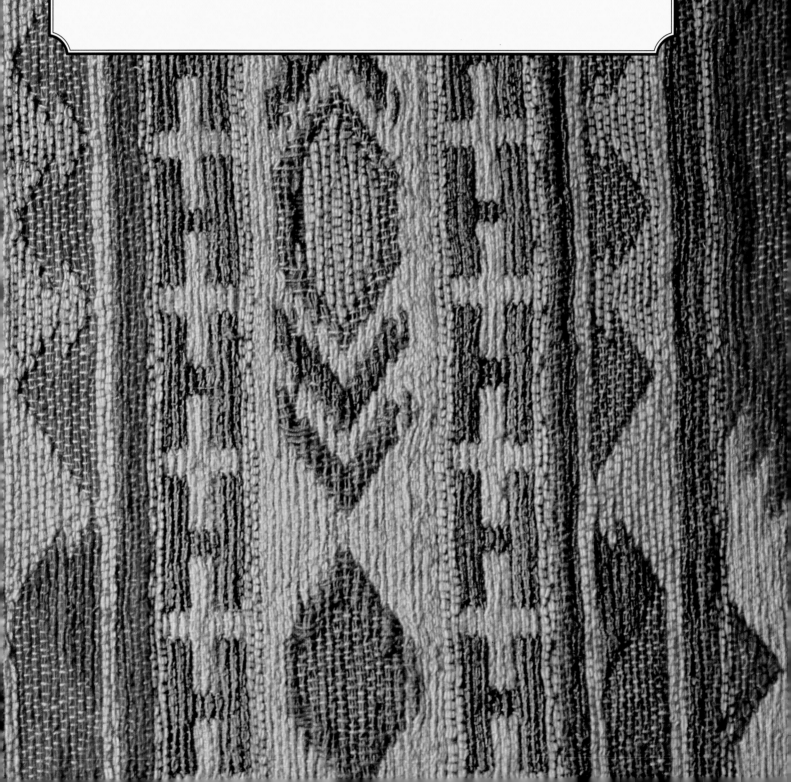

INTRODUCTION

More and more people are discovering the pleasure of making things for themselves. Not only is it a delight to create a beautiful object, but using your spare time to make something attractive and useful is enormously satisfying.

As we are increasingly surrounded by mass-produced objects, there is a natural reaction to return to the simpler, more traditional skills of our forebears. Moreover, much of what can be created may be done inexpensively or with recycled materials, providing an easy means of creating unique, personal gifts and decorating living space.

The crafts and techniques described can all be done at home. Most need no special tools or equipment, but can be carried out with the materials and implements to be found in almost every home needlework box or tool box. For beginners and experts alike there are many simple projects, illustrated with step-by-step instructions, that offer practical and informed guidance to using the techniques explained throughout the book. There is something beautiful and useful here for the whole family, either to be made, or to be given with the true delight and satisfaction of the creator.

Evenweave fabrics are available in a range of colors and counts. Samplers are traditionally worked on cream or beige background fabrics, so keep your deep-dyed fabrics and pastel shades for other projects.

Opposite: The variety of patterns, materials, finishes and trims that can be used on a basic 12in (30cm) square cushion cover is limitless. They are also a good way of using up left-over furnishing fabrics.

Right: These little white hearts are being used to create a dainty appliqué motif. The close buttonhole stitch is in a contrasting color, but white would be just as pretty. If you have a sewing hoop, use it to hold the base fabric taut – it will make your task much easier.

Hexagons are often used for patchwork piecing. The traditional pattern Grandmother's Flower Garden uses rosettes of hexagons held together with strips of, often, plain hexagons, but whether you prefer a random effect or a more structured pattern, choose your colors with care so that strong, glowing shades contrast with, but do not clash with or overpower, more delicate patterns and colors.

Shells make an attractive surround for this plain mirror, but you could use pretty pebbles or even colorful glass nuggets.

There are so many different materials and patterns in basket making that it would be possible to work for a lifetime and never make the same piece twice. This is a rewarding and fascinating craft – and you will never lack gifts for your friends and family.

Salt dough need not be used just for brightly colored, spaghetti-haired trolls. This basket is both attractive and useful, virtues not always associated with salt dough.

NEEDLECRAFT

Opposite: Use small pieces of canvas and your left-over tapestry wools to make a cosy for your tea pot. Base your design on your own tea set or on one by the famous nineteenth-century tea-ware manufacturers such as Minton, whose pattern books contain a wealth of inspirational designs.

There are so many traditional skills associated with stitching and fabrics that anyone who is at all handy with a needle and who enjoys sewing and working with silks, cottons and wools can furnish an entire home, from duvet cover to curtains, from decorated towels to egg-cosies. Craft shops and haberdashery sections of even fairly modestly sized department stores stock almost anything you might need – and a lot more besides.

Needlepoint

Of all needlecrafts, needlepoint is deservedly the most popular. There are so many wonderful colors available in the huge ranges of stranded cottons and tapestry wools and such a variety of evenweave fabrics and mono canvases that it would be difficult not to find a medium that you enjoy working in. It is also a versatile medium, permitting you to create an enormous range of finished articles, and the end results are not only hard-wearing but practical as well.

Most craft shops and mail order suppliers now offer an enormous selection of kits and of pre-printed canvas and evenweave fabric designs, and there can be few stitchers who have not succumbed to the temptation of a printed canvas or easy-to-follow chart, pre-packaged with selected wools or stranded cottons. Even if you do not want to buy a kit, you can find printed canvases for simple, stylized animals and toys, worked in cross stitch with rug wool on canvas, or even copies of old masters, ready to be worked in cross stitch, tent stitch or half cross stitch with the wool or cottons of your choice. Glance along the shelves of your local bookshop and you will find dozens of books with charts to follow for all manner of designs. There are flowers, borders, animals, birds and butterflies to stitch on any type of fabric you care to mention. Whether your preference is for an easy cross stitch design worked in wool on canvas or for a delicate motif worked in a single strand of embroidery cotton on the finest of evenweave fabrics, you will find a book with the appropriate charts to follow.

Even if you cannot immediately find a motif or pattern that you like, look at your curtain and carpets to see if you can adapt the motifs and designs to a design for your needlepoint canvas or evenweave. Graph paper and some crayons or felt-tipped pens are all you need to work out a new chart. Remembering that one square on the graph paper represents a single stitch, plan your design. Oriental rugs and carpets are a wonderful source of inspiration for geometric designs, which can be simplified and adapted to suit your own furnishing style and stitching abilities. If you have a painting or picture that you especially like, work a piece in bargello (see page 23) to complement or contrast with the colors.

If you would prefer a pictorial design but are not sufficiently confident of your skills as an artist to create your own, you can easily transfer a photograph or picture to charted paper. Most craft shops now stock tracing paper that has a grid printed on it, and it is available in a variety of grid sizes, from 10- to 22-count, corresponding to the count sizes of evenweave fabrics. The more detail you want to add to your design, the higher the count you should use. If you have access to a light box or have a glass-topped table under which you can fix a light source, you can use ordinary graph paper.

The wonderfully vivid flowers on this cushion cover are a fine example of free-style embroidery. The petals and leaves are worked in satin stitch, which creates a smooth, rich appearance.

Decide on the size you want for the finished design and draw the dimensions on the graph paper. Use a photocopier to enlarge or reduce the photograph or illustration to the appropriate size and use masking tape to hold it in place under the graph paper. Then, all you have to do is go over the lines of the design on the graph paper. If you are planning to work in cross stitch, the outlines will have to be squared up. Half cross stitch and tent stitch allow you a little more flexibility with angles. When you are happy with the outline and have drawn in all the main features, use crayons or felt-tipped pens to add the details. This method is especially useful if you want to transfer a photograph of your house to needlepoint.

There are only a few simple rules to observe to ensure complete success with every project. Keep your work in a plastic bag or sewing bag when you are not actually stitching. Not only will this help to keep your work clean, but it will also keep all the shades you are using for one project together. It may seem obvious, but it is worth cutting a short length of each shade of tapestry wool or stranded cotton and attaching each one to a card with the appropriate symbol (if you are working from a chart) and manufacturer's shade number written next to it. Use an ordinary hole punch to make a series of holes in an old greetings card so that you have a full record of all the shades you have used, together with the reference number, for a particular project. This is especially useful if you are working on more than one piece at a time, and it is also a vital reference if you want to repeat the design later on, perhaps to make another matching cushion cover or additional sets of curtain-ties.

Make sure that you use the appropriate needle. When you are working with wool, use a tapestry needle with a blunt point and a large eye so that you can insert the point between threads without piercing the wool in the previous row. When you are working on evenweave fabric, choose a needle of which the eye is not so large that it distorts that fabric as you push and pull it through. Do not leave your needle in the design area of the work. Even the best quality needles can mark your work, and rust stains are impossible to remove.

Although it may seem unnecessarily tedious, if you are using stranded cottons, cut a length and separate the six strands, smoothing them on a pad before threading your needle with the number of strands you require. The finished work looks smoother and more even. If you are working with wool, run your fingers lightly along a length and you will find that there is a "right" and a "wrong" way. Stitch so that the fibres in the wool are pulled smooth as it passes through the holes of the canvas.

Whether you use a frame is very much a matter of personal preference, and it is often much easier to work small pieces in the hand. Some people, however, always use a frame or hoop, and there can be no doubt that it can make your work easier and improve the finished appearance. When evenweave fabric is held taut in an embroidery or tambour hoop, it is much easier to insert the needle cleanly through the holes. Bind the hoops with masking tape, not only to protect the fabric from being marked but also to prevent it from slipping. Large pieces of canvas are most easily worked when the canvas is held in a frame. The best kind are the old-fashioned slate frames, which have two side bars and two cross-bars. The canvas is

Opposite: Making cushion covers is one of the easiest and best ways of introducing color and personal style to your home. There is hardly any limit on the variety of patterns and colors that can be used, whether you prefer a more traditional floral pattern, such as this one, or something more modern and colorful.

Opposite: Although it looks easy, this number sampler is a fine example of a needleworker's skill. Its charm lies in the restrained use of color and the careful balancing of the different kinds of numerals chosen. Remember to use non-reflective glass when you frame your handiwork and make sure that it is displayed out of direct sunlight.

stitched to strips of fabric attached to the cross-bars, which are held firm to the side bars by wing nuts. Because the canvas is wound around the cross-bars, a frame can accommodate a range of lengths. If you do not have a slate frame, use artists' stretcher bars, and pin your canvas to the wooden framework. Floor-mounted frames are also available, or you can use a frame that can be clamped to a table.

Do not begin or end your work with knots. When you start a new length of wool or cotton, hold down the end under the first four or five stitches. When you finish, thread the working strand under four or five stitches. Snip off loose ends close to the back of the work. Do not carry strands from one area of your work to another. If you are working on a light evenweave fabric, the carried thread may be visible from the front, and a long, loose thread on the back of your work may easily get caught up with your working thread and cause knots.

Although cross stitch is usually worked on evenweave fabric, the appearance in craft shops of disposable waste canvas has made stitching designs on to all kinds of materials so simple that it is tempting to use it on everything, but especially children's clothes and bed and table linen.

For a fairly simple motif you will need waste canvas in a suitable count, basting thread, stranded embroidery cotton, a pair of tweezers and some water in a spray-bottle. Decide on the finished size of your chosen design and cut out a piece of waste canvas that is about $1\frac{1}{2}$in (4cm) larger all around than the finished motif. Align the blue threads in the waste canvas vertically or horizontally with the weave of your chosen fabric or, if you want to stitch directly to a finished garment, line up a blue line with a seam. Pin, then baste the waste canvas in position. It is a good idea to baste diagonally across as well as around the edge of the canvas so that it cannot move while you work and to make certain that the underlying fabric is smooth and held close to the waste canvas. Remove the pins before you begin. Stitch your chosen motif, treating each pair of canvas threads as a single thread, but otherwise working as you would on any other evenweave fabric and beginning and finishing off threads on the underneath in the normal way. If a piece is going to be washed often, you might for a change want to make a knot in the end of your cotton. Complete the motif, then trim away the excess canvas, leaving about $\frac{1}{2}$in (1cm) all round. Taking care not to soak your work, spray the embroidery from the front lightly with warm water. You are aiming to dampen it sufficiently for the size in the canvas to soften so that you can remove the strands of canvas with the tweezers. This is a rather laborious task because you have to remove one strand at a time. If you try to pull out several strands at the same time, you will spoil your work. If the material you have worked on has to be dry cleaned, gently rub the canvas, which should loosen the threads so that you can pull them out. When you have finished, press the work lightly from the wrong side.

When you are working in cross stitch the only rule to observe is that the top stitch of every cross slants in the same direction. Whether you prefer to work a row of half stitches across an area of your design and then work back, stitching the top half of the cross, or whether you prefer to complete each stitch as you go is entirely a personal choice.

Tent stitch, which is sometimes also called continental stitch, is often

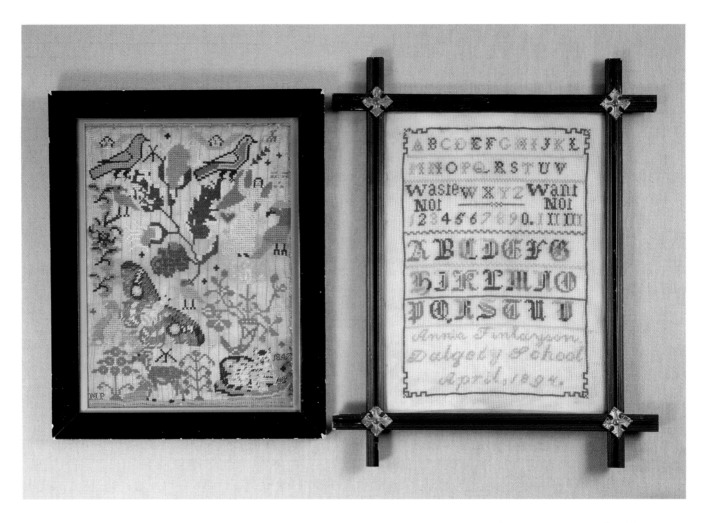

Traditionally, samplers were nothing more than a way of recording different stitches. As time passed, they came to be used to record a stitcher's prowess and, later, specific events in a family's life. The sampler on the left, which bears the initials MP and the date 1847, reveals the workings of a whimsical imagination – a giant butterfly flaps above a greedy goat, while the fat cat bears more than a passing resemblance to the china dogs that used to adorn mantelpieces. Above them are exotic plants and birds. The sampler on the right, which bears the date 1894, has been stitched with a moralizing proverb, but the colorful gothic letters suggest that the stitcher had more artistic leanings or, perhaps, was simply putting into practice with the left-over silks the improving words that had been so carefully worked.

preferred for needlepoint worked in wool on canvas, especially if the finished project is going to be made up into something that is subject to wear, such as a cushion cover. It covers exceptionally well and produces a dense, hard-wearing surface. When you are working a horizontal row from right to left, bring the needle up through a lower left square, take it to the back through the diagonally opposite upper right square and bring it to the front through the hole to the left of the first hole, passing under two vertical threads on the back of your work. You will create a short diagonal on the front of your work, but a long diagonal on the back. Turn your work and stitch back in the same way. If you need to work a horizontal row from left to right bring your needle to the front through a hole in the upper row, take it to the back through the diagonally opposite lower left hole, and bring it to the front through the hole to the right of the first hole.

When it is worked horizontally or vertically for large areas, tent stitch does tend to distort and pull canvases out of shape, so if you are not using a frame you might prefer to use diagonal or basketweave tent stitch for background areas. Working from the top left of your canvas, bring your needle to the front through a lower left square, take it to the back through the diagonally opposite upper right square and bring it back to the front through the square diagonally below the first square – that is, under two threads of the canvas and vertically down from the second square. You will have a short diagonal stitch on the front of your work but a long vertical stitch on the back. Continue to work towards the bottom right in the same way. Do not turn your work. Beginning at bottom right, bring the needle to the front through a lower left-hand hole and take it to the back through the diagonally opposite upper right hole. Bring it to the front through the hole diagonally up from the first hole – that is, the thread passes horizontally under two threads of the canvas. This stitch gives a neat, basketweave appearance on the back of your work, and it is a firm, hard-wearing stitch that is ideal for cushion covers.

One of the most attractive techniques for cushion covers, chair seats and curtain tie-backs is bargello, which is also known as Florentine stitch, flame stitch, Hungarian stitch and Irish stitch. Bargello, which is best worked on canvas, is basically a series of vertical stitches worked over horizontal rows of the canvas to create a wave pattern. The flexibility of the stitch lies in the fact that the pattern you work and colors your choose can be as dramatic or as subtle as you wish.

At its simplest, bargello is made by working a vertical stitch over four horizontal rows of the canvas. The next stitch, parallel to the first, begins a horizontal row higher and ends a horizontal row higher, and so on until five or six vertical stitches have been worked. The next stitch is one horizontal row lower and so on, until you are stitching into the same horizontal row as your first stitch. Then you begin to work upwards again. When you have finished the wave row across the canvas, use the second color to work another row directly above it. Every stitch will share its holes with the stitches directly above and directly below it.

There are numerous variations on the basic stitch. The wave can be made shallower or deeper; you can work two or more stitches at the same depth before moving to the next row on your canvas; you can make some of the stitches longer than others in the row; you can vary the depth between stitches by beginning vertical stitches two rows above the previous stitch; you can work irregularly angled waves; you can create curves by working blocks of stitches at the same depth; you can work so that the pattern is symmetrical or asymmetrical. The possibilities are practically endless. You can make your work look strikingly modern by using strong, brightly contrasting colors, or you can make it look slightly old-fashioned and understated by using shades of the same color or close tones of different colors. The other great advantage of bargello work is that, once you have established the pattern by working your first row across the canvas, your work will grow very quickly. It is also the ideal needlepoint to work while you are half-watching television because you do not have to count squares or keep referring to a chart.

Samplers

Samplers were, it is thought, first worked in Germany or Italy in the late fifteenth century. These early pieces were worked in a single color, and they were intended more for future reference than as decorative objects. Samplers traditionally had no worked background. The designs and stitches were worked on long, narrow strips of fabric, about 25 x 9in (60 x 23cm). In the days before pattern books were available they were regarded as a convenient way of keeping together a record of worked embroidery stitches

Above: Nowadays, samplers are often stitched to commemorate a special event, and there can be few more personal ways of recording a birth. Samplers worked with love and care today will be the treasures and heirlooms of tomorrow.

Opposite: A sampler worked to celebrate a wedding will be a lasting reminder of a happy day. When working a sampler with names and figures such as this, carefully plan your design on graph paper so the lettering and design are in the middle of the fabric and the border pattern meets neatly in the corners.

and techniques, and they were not planned. Some of the oldest examples reveal how a stitcher's skills developed over the years, from using simple cross stitch to work letters and numbers to being able to work complicated open work patterns and a variety of new stitches.

Later, samplers were used as a way of showing off the stitcher's skills. Improving verses were often worked, and borders and motifs were copied from the pattern books that became available in the eighteenth century. As linen became more widely available, different widths could be used, and samplers became squarer.

These days samplers are often worked to mark a special occasion, such as a wedding or a christening, when they include names and dates as well as attractive borders and motifs such as bells or little flowers. Simple samplers,

Opposite: Succulent, toothsome olives, crisp, fresh bread and red wine are the perfect snack for a sunny day. And the perfect finishing touch – hand-embroidered napkins.

including the alphabet or numbers separated by patterned borders can be equally attractive, and because the background is not worked, they do not take too long to complete.

For best results, use graph paper to plan your sampler. The proportions and spacing of letters and figures are surprisingly difficult to work out, so it is well worth looking for some ready-charted letters from a book and adapting them to your own requirements. If you are working a sampler to mark a change of address, you might want to include an image of the new house. Use the photocopying technique described earlier in this chapter, but simplify and stylize the outline.

Use an evenweave fabric or a mono (not interlock) canvas. If you use evenweave, choose 26- or 29-count ecru or white. If you prefer to use canvas, choose a pale cream base with a 16, 18 or 24 mesh; avoid the dark ecru colored canvas, which looks unimaginably unattractive when it is not completely covered with stitches.

Samplers are usually worked in cross stitch with stranded cotton or crewel wool, but – in keeping with their traditional function – you might use the opportunity of working a sampler to try out some of the variations on the basic theme. Upright cross stitch, for example, is worked with horizontal and vertical stitches instead of diagonal ones. Complete each stitch in turn, and remember that all the top stitches of every cross should be vertical or horizontal, but not a mixture of the two. Crossed corner stitch is worked with a large diagonal cross over four threads of the fabric, with short diagonal stitches worked over the points of the large cross. Gobelin stitch can be worked over two, three or four threads of canvas. It is a straight stitch, which is useful for edgings or for working in blocks. At corners you can make a fan-shaped stitch by working five stitches into the same hole on the inner side, but taking the thread through to the back into five adjacent holes, the longest stitch being the third, which is used to turn the corner.

One of the most delightful features of antique samplers is the subtlety of the colors that were used. It is only recently that synthetic dyes have been used for embroidery cottons and tapestry wools, and if you feel that some of the cottons and tapestry wools in your sewing box are rather too garish to do full justice to your sampler design, you should try dyeing your own wools. Some specialist dye suppliers are now producing their own ranges of vegetable dyes. However, before you buy spend money on a commercially produced dye, consider making your own. Animal fibres – silk, wool and mohair – and vegetable fibres – cotton and linen – can be dyed easily at home, and you will have an even greater sense of achievement if you use plants from your own garden. Begin with tapestry wools, which accept vegetables dyes better than cottons, although if you are feeling adventurous you may be pleasantly surprised at the results you achieve with cotton. You must wash the yarn thoroughly before you attempt to dye it to remove all residues of chemical treatments.

Most of the shades that can be achieved by using plants are tones of yellow, green and brown. Mrs Grieve notes that the flowers of marigold (*Calendula officinalis*), which used to be used to give cheese a yellow color, can be boiled to produce a golden-yellow dye, while a decoction

It is far easier to buy ready-made table linen onto which you can embroider your own motifs than to buy lengths of linen, which you then have to cut and hem. Dye white table linen to match your decor, then let your guests know how much you value them by working a simple design such as these dainty daisies for a special dinner party.

made of the leaves of the common nettle (*Urticaria dioica*): "yields a beautiful and permanent green dye, which is used for woollen stuffs in Russia." She also says that the roots of nettles will provide a yellow dye, used in medieval England to dye yarn yellow and in Russia to stain eggs for Maundy Thursday. Elderberry (*Sambucus nigra*) is an especially versatile plant: the berries give blue and purple dye and the berry juice alone gives violet, the leaves yields green, and the bark can be used to produce black. Like the purple dye from other berries, however, the dye from elderberries is prone to turning brown. Leaves such as walnut and dock produce a light brown shade, while walnut hulls give a much darker, warmer brown.

Before you begin, remember that you must use a mordant if the dyes are to fix properly. Rhubarb leaves, which produce a dye themselves (it is yellowish), contain oxalic acid, a natural mordant that can be used with other colors. Rhubarb leaves are, of course, poisonous, so handle them carefully. An alternative is alum, a chemical that is widely available in chemists, mixed with cream of tartar. Other mordants that can be tried include tannic acid, lemon juice, white vinegar and the leaves of the staghorn sumach (*Rhus typhina*). Using different mordants affects the dye in different ways, with iron tending to produce lighter shades and alum darker tones.

Simmer the pre-washed yarn in the mordant for about 45 minutes before

you attempt to dye it. Use your plant materials fresh or dry, boiling them in water for up to an hour. Strain the liquid, then add the a damp yarn. Simmer again. Rinse and wash thoroughly before allowing to dry naturally.

Embroidery

Although cross stitch, half cross stitch and tent stitch and the associated variations can be used in dozens of different ways, you do need to work on evenweave fabric. There may be occasions when you will want to work on a plainweave, and this is when the whole range of embroidery stitches comes into its own. There are, quite literally hundreds of embroidery stitches that can be used, and they can all be used to create different effects. The most often used are described below, but encyclopedias of stitches contain many, many more.

Stem stitch, which is useful for outlining motifs or, as the name suggests, for gently curved lines, is worked backwards along a single line from left to right. Bring your needle through to the right side of the fabric and take it through to the back a short distance to the right, holding your needle so that it is pointing to your left at a slight angle. Bring your needle through to the front about halfway along your first stitch and to one side of it. Keep all your stitches on the top the same size and always bring your needle to the

There can be few more delicious scents than freshly brewed coffee mingling with the buttery smell of warm, crumbly croissants. Make napkins from an easy-to-wash cotton-mix fabric and use your sewing machine to stitch a simple scallop edge in a contrasting shade.

An elegant white scalloped edge is the only decoration needed on this fine cotton tea tray. Work close buttonhole stitch by hand or save time and use your machine.

right side of the fabric on the left-hand side of the previous stitch. Stem stitch can be whipped (when a contrasting color is passed through each stitch without going through the fabric) or threaded (when a contrasting color is woven in and out of the stitches to create an undulating row).

Satin stitch is used to fill shapes such as petals. Work from left to right, bringing your needle through to the front on the very edge of the shape to be filled. Take the needle to the back on the opposite edge, then bring it back to the front as close as possible to the first stitch. Your stitches should be as close together as possible, but they should lie evenly and smoothly. Do not pull the thread too tight and use an embroidery hoop so that the fabric is not pulled out of shape. Padded satin stitch is sometimes used to give extra depth to embroidery. Work around the edge of the shape with tiny running stitches and fill the centre of the shape with scattered stitches before oversewing the shape with satin stitch.

Herringbone stitch is not just a useful decorative stitch – it can also be worked when you need to hold down a turned raw edge in situations when normal hemming is not appropriate. The stitch is worked from left to right. Hold your needle so that it points to the right and make a small, horizontal running stitch. Bring out the needle and, still with it pointing to the right, make a second horizontal running stitch, the same size as the first stitch about 1/4in (5mm) below and parallel to it but slightly to the right. Make the next step on the same line as the first but slightly to the right of the second. On the back of your work you will have two parallel rows of running stitches. On the front you will have overlapping diagonal lines.

French knots and straight stitch are used to fill outlines with random stitches. To work a French knot bring your needle to the front and, if you are right handed, hold the thread in your left hand. Twist the needle so that the thread is twisted (do not, as is often suggested, twist the thread around the needle) and take the needle to the back of your work close to where it emerges so that the twisted thread lies neatly on the surface of your work. Straight stitch is basically individual satin stitches worked in any direction. Although they can be any length, they look neater if they are not too long and if they are pretty much the same length. Try to avoid carrying the thread for long distances on the wrong side of your work. Couching involves laying a thread along a line and using small, evenly spaced stitches to hold it in place.

Opposite: Fine table linen is always a pleasure to own and use. Here, delicate embroidery silks have been used with the drawn thread technique to make a pretty cloth for tea on a summer afternoon.

Project
Embroidered Monogram

One of the nicest ways of personalizing table and bed linen is to embroider your own initials or, on a gift, those of the recipient in a corner. Many of us can no doubt remember laboriously back stitching or stem stitching an initial into the corner of a handkerchief for a Father's Day gift. Here, we have used a cursive style of lettering and worked in a contrasting cotton. The finished piece has then been lightly padded and appliquéd to a pocket. On ordinary linen, however, you might prefer to work with white on white, which is both traditional and attractive.

1. Trace from an alphabet in the style of your choice the letters you want to stitch. If you are not certain about the spacing, trace the letters on to two pieces of paper so that you can experiment with their relative positions. When you are happy with the result, copy the letters on to a single sheet.

2. Transfer the initial letters to the fabric. We used dressmaker's carbon, but if you have a light box you could go over the lines with a washable marker.

3. If you wish, stitch the outline of the letters in tiny running stitches. Use satin stitch to fill in the letters, keeping your stitches even and smooth. An embroidery hoop will help prevent the fabric from puckering as you work.

4. Use a small square of lightweight wadding and make sure that, when you turn under the hem around the initials, your embroidery is positioned exactly in the centre of the square. Carefully press down the hem, taking care that you do not flatten the stitches, and either machine stitch or sew in place with tiny slip stitches.

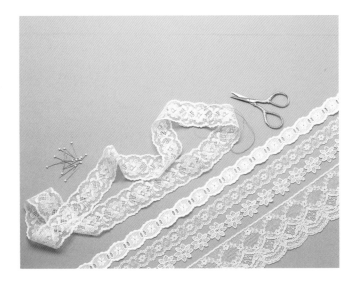

Lace-making, Crochet and Tatting

Antique lace is among the most beautiful of all hand-crafted materials. There are two main kinds – needlepoint and bobbin lace. Machine-made lace first appeared in the late eighteenth-century, and although today we can walk into haberdashery shops and buy lengths of machine-made lace, nineteenth-century machine-made lace is well worth looking out for. Many lace-like materials can be produced in other ways, including crocheting, tatting and knotting, and knitting can be used to produce delicate, lacy things.

Needlepoint lace is, as the name suggests, made with an ordinary sewing needle and a single thread, largely with buttonhole stitch. However, when we think of lace, most of us are referring to bobbin lace, which is also known as pillow lace and bone work. It is made by plaiting and twisting large numbers of the threads, wound separately on to bobbins, over a parchment pattern on a pillow. Up to 30 pairs of bobbins are required to make a simple edging, while a wide piece of lace may require as many as 500 pairs. There are many different styles, and learning to identify the subtle variations between French, English and Belgian laces is a lifetime's work. We can all recognize the quality and beauty of a delicately worked motif or edging, however.

Top left: Machine-made lace is available in a wide range of patterns and weights. A simple border on a pillowcase or table cloth can make the ordinary very special.

Top right: Once you have the knack, crochet is an easy craft to pursue. Use crochet cotton and a fine steel hook to create all manner of pretty articles.

Above left: Tatting shuttles come in a variety of sizes and shapes, but you have to wind your working thread on to the shuttle before you begin. You will also need a hook – and it is helpful to pin the worked piece on to a padded surface before lightly pressing it.

Above right: More complex looking pieces of tatting are worked with picots, by which individual motifs can be held together. Make sure that all your stitches are the same size and that you do not pull them too tight, or the finished piece will not lie flat.

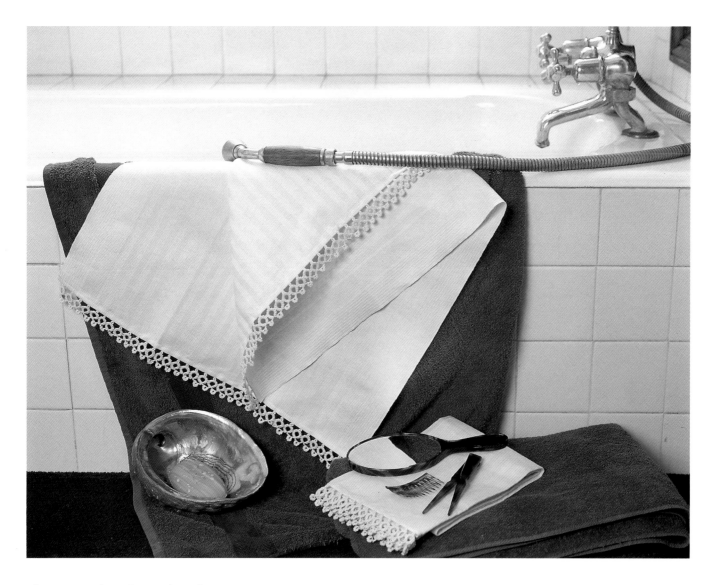

Above: A tatting trim on these linen guest towels transforms a plain and serviceable article into something special and luxurious.

Right: Search through antique shops and charity shops for hand-made lace attached to old clothes and bed and table linen. Always wash lace by hand in soap (not a harsh detergent) and dry it carefully, away from direct heat.

A very simple but effective example of crochet – this simplest of techniques can appear both delicate and complex but need not take long to make.

Small pieces of antique lace, whether hand-made or machine-made, can add an indefinable character to plain table linen or to a dressing-table runner. Look out for old tablecloths and even garments in antique shops and in second-hand shops. You may throw away the article to which the lace was attached, but spend time carefully unpicking the lace, washing it by hand and pressing it gently under a cloth.

Few of us are likely to have the time or patience required to plan and work a piece of bobbin lace, but two related crafts – crochet and tatting – are well within the scope of the home needleworker.

Crochet is, perhaps, the simplest of all possible handicrafts. Once you have mastered the basic stitch – and there really is only one – you will

Even your Christmas decorations can be given that personal touch. This little angel was made from a practice piece of tatting.

You do not have to work in a single color when you have gained experience with crochet. This colorful table mat shows what a versatile craft it is and why it is now enjoying something of a revival.

Above: When they are used on a polished wooden floor, remember to attach a few small grippers to the back of your rug so that it does not slip and cause accidents.

Left: Ensure that the plaits are smooth and even. If you pull the plaits too tightly, your rug will not curl neatly together and if they are too loose, it will look untidy.

Opposite: Rag rugs can be made in whatever colors you wish. Make sure the fabrics you use are pre-shrunk and that they are all pretty much the same weight – then away you go.

quickly be able to make some really pretty things, working in rounds or backwards and forwards across rows, making shells, diadem stitches, sunrise stitches, single tulips, double tulips – the possibilities are almost endless, yet they can all be worked from the same simple stitch. Unfortunately, crochet seems to have become inextricably linked with afghan throws. These are, undeniably, a quick and cheerful way of using up odds and ends of wool, but crochet can be used to far better effect than for making a brightly colored patchwork blanket that does not suit any of your indoor decorations. And anyway, your cat is sure to find the only loose end you have left and will quickly unravel your carefully stitched together squares.

Use a fine steel hook to work with very fine cotton, silk or linen yarn and keep your larger aluminium hooks for wools and synthetic yarns. Look around for crochet patterns that use unstranded crochet cotton or coton perle. Filet crochet, in which trebles and chains are used to build up a pattern in meshes of solid and open squares, can be particularly attractive in an understated way. Work pretty lacy edgings for table linen and bed linen in fine white cotton or use a strongly contrasting color.

Do not throw away your large crochet hooks. Use them with bias-cut strips of cotton fabrics, stitched or knotted together. Work in rounds and you will make a rug for, say a bathroom or child's room, in no time at all. These rugs can be easily washed or, because they take so little effort to make, replaced when you get tired of them.

Tatting, which shares some characteristics with knotting, can be used to make dainty edgings or entire pieces. It is thought to have developed in Britain in the nineteenth century, although it was originally used in Italy as early as the sixteenth century. Tatting is worked with the same kinds of cotton as fine crochet, but you need one or two shuttles, on to which the thread is wound, and a picot hook (or a fine crochet hook). There are three stitches – a single stitch, a double stitch and a picot – and these are worked over a running thread and then pulled up into rings or left as chain bars. The single stitch resembles buttonhole stitch, and the picots are loops of thread left between double stitches. Once mastered it is a rather soothing craft, but it grows slowly, so begin with a fairly small-scale project – the edging to a tea tray, perhaps – until you can work without really thinking.

Two embroidery techniques can also be used as time-saving alternatives to making real lace – pulled thread work and drawn thread work. Both techniques need to be worked on evenweave fabric. Pulled thread work is a kind of counted thread embroidery. In it, embroidery stitches are pulled tight to create open areas on the background fabric. Geometric patterns work best, although you can use the technique for pictorial designs. The more open the weave of the fabric you use, the airier and more dainty will be the finished effect.

Drawn thread work, which is quite different from pulled thread work, involves removing entire threads from a piece of fabric. Choose a fairly open weave and lift the appropriate thread with the point of a needle. Use your smallest, sharpest scissors to snip the thread and carefully pull it out. The difficulty arises when you need to turn a corner. Mark the point with a pin and cut both the warp and the weft threads (the horizontal and vertical threads), gently pulling them out as far as the next corner. Carefully darn in

Opposite: Cut-work always looks cool and crisp. The designs, which can be geometric or free style, are outlined in a small running stitch before worked with a neat, close buttonhole stitch. The fabric is then carefully cut away. The lacy effect can be enhanced by stitching buttonhole bars across large open areas. This technique, known as renaissance work, has an especially delicate appearance.

Project
Plaited Rag Rug

Lightweight towelling is ideal for this kind of rug, and clear yellow and white make a rug that would be perfect for a bathroom or sunny kitchen. Towelling is easy to work with and easy to wash, but the beauty of these rugs is that almost any kind of material can be used.

1. Cut strips about 2in (5cm) wide and approximately 12in (30cm) long and fold and pin the raw edges inwards.

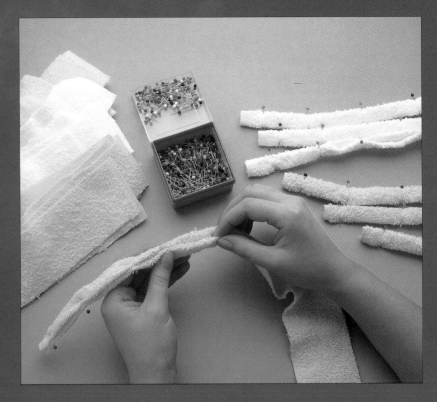

2. Use your sewing machine to stitch along the open edge, keeping your stitches as near to the edge as you can.

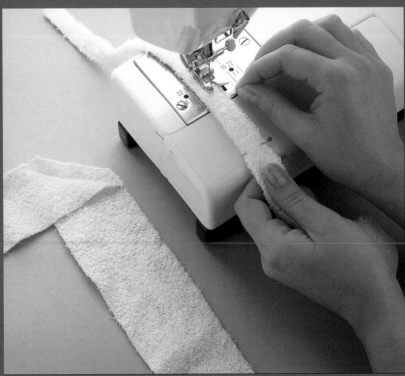

3. Join several strips together as you work and turning in the raw edges to make invisible seams, and make the strips of one color (yellow, here) into a piece twice as long as the white strip. At first, you will should join about three white strips and six yellow strips.

4. Pin the white strip in the centre of the long yellow strip.

5. When you are beginning the plait, it is often easier to pin the strips to a piece of hardboard or a cork tile, so that both hands are free.

6. Begin to plait the three strands together. Do not make the plait too tight, and keep the strands from twisting as you work so that the plait is the same width throughout.

7. Add more strips to the end of the plait. You will find it easier to keep the plait flat and even if you add each new strip at an angle of 90 degrees to the previous piece.

8. Thread a double length of strong thread on a bodkin and begin to stitch the plait together, coiling it carefully on itself.

9. Work from the back and take the thread through the centre of the plait each time. Do not pull the thread so tight that the rug will not lie flat, but do not leave it so loose that the plait is not held firmly together.

10. Overstitch the raw ends neatly to the previous row.

the loose ends so that they will not fray. The embroidery stitches are worked over the threads that are left. Drawn thread work can be used to make pretty, open borders to table cloths and table mats, and if you wish, you can thread narrow ribbon through the remaining threads, interlacing it to create a pretty, lace-like effect.

Rag Rugs

Lace, drawn thread work and tatting are at the opposite end of the handi-craft scale to rag rugs, but both crafts are equally satisfying in their own ways. Making rag rugs is a wonderful way of recycling unwanted fabrics or outgrown clothes. There are three main methods – plaiting, knotting, which is similar to crochet, and hooking. Hooked rugs require a backing of sturdy canvas, but plaited and knotted rugs do not.

Although you can – indeed, you should – use whatever materials come to hand, the Shakers, who first made these plaited and coiled rugs, preferred to use shades of a single color or similar tones. If you are buying fabrics especially to plait into a rug, choose warm browns and terracottas or blues and grays. Woollen materials work well, and you can mix together in a single rug fabrics of different textures as long as they are all of a similar weight. Remember to pre-shrink all fabrics before use.

Rag rugs tends to rely more on texture than on design or images to achieve their effects. If you are particularly interested in pictorial rugs, consider using a tufting gun or, more traditionally, a large cross stitch on strong canvas.

Hooked rugs are made from long strips of fabric, no more than 3/4in (2cm) wide, which are held at the back of the canvas and pulled through to the front with a hook (a large, strong crochet hook will do). Each loop is left uncut, so that the whole surface of the rug is eventually covered with small, even loops. Use natural fibres – wool and cotton – for the best results. The technique lends itself equally well to geometric and pictorial rugs.

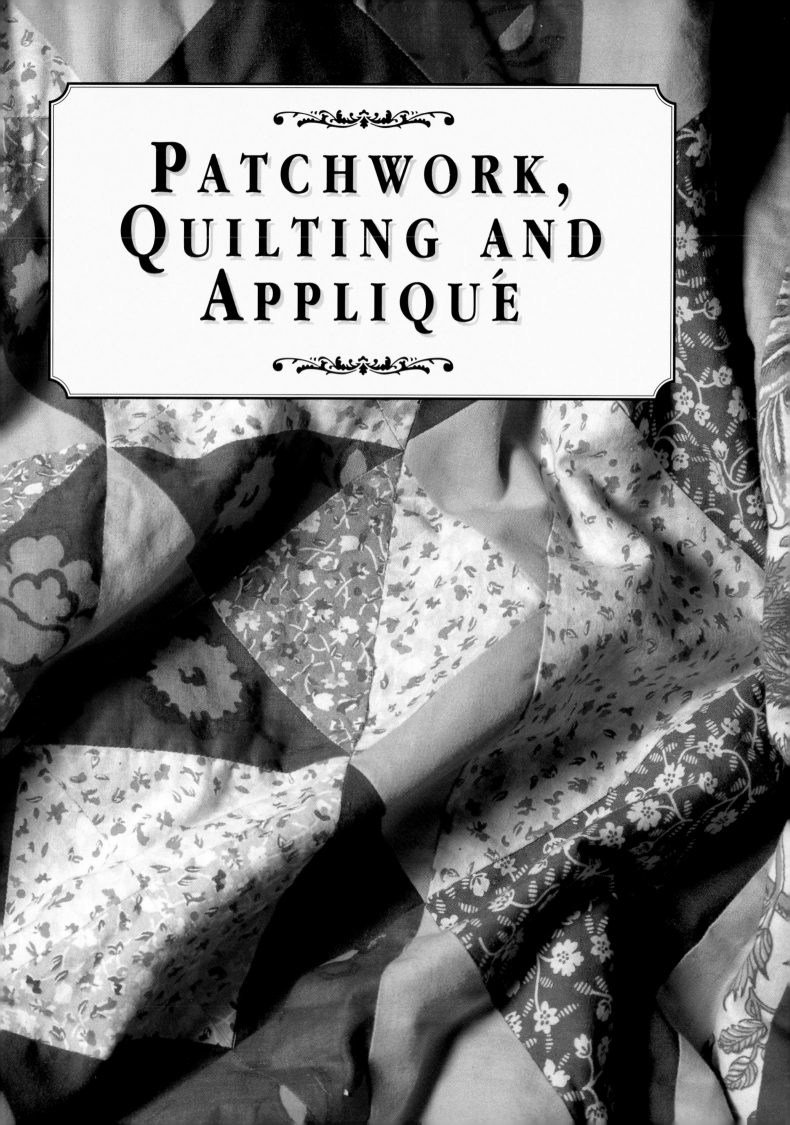

PATCHWORK, QUILTING AND APPLIQUÉ

Opposite: Craft shops and the haberdashery sections of department stores stock a range of templates, and it is worth taking time over the marking and cutting out of the pieces so that the angles fit perfectly together. When you get bitten by the patchwork bug, invest in a rotary cutter, which will make your life infinitely easier.

Overleaf: Bright clear red and clean white are a wonderful contrast, used to great effect in this simple pieced patchwork cushion cover.

Below: Patchwork was traditionally a way of using scraps of left-over fabric, but sophisticated designs such as this are best worked in carefully selected shades. The very nature of patchwork is of masses of small pieces, but if you want to achieve a coordinated effect, buy lengths of fabric especially for each project. Remember to pre-wash them before use, however, to pre-shrink them and to check that the colors will not run and spoil your handiwork.

Those three associated crafts are enjoying an enormous revival. Patchwork has, of course, never "gone away", and discerning collectors have long been seeking out hand-pieced quilts from the nineteenth century and the early decades of the present century. The glowing colors of Amish quilts have inspired many a needleworker and have set standards to which many aspire. Craft shops now stock everything that is needed, from charting paper, iron-on interfacing and templates to fabrics in shades and patterns that were unimaginable only a few years ago. As we use our sewing machines and rotary cutters we should, perhaps, spare a thought for stitchers who worked by hand with paper and card templates and scraps of material to create those works of art that we now seek to emulate.

Patchwork

Patchwork is the traditional way of using up scraps of unwanted cottons, silks and other fabrics. It has developed from an ancient technique that is almost coeval with man's earliest clothes, and the process involves using left-over pieces of material either to make complete garments or articles or to decorate or disguise worn places on favourite clothes.

Among the earliest makers of patchwork were the Pilgrim Fathers and settlers in North America. Because large quantities of new fabrics were not available, they used scraps from their old clothes to make whole garments and household furnishings. It was from this tradition that arose the

Previous page 55: If you decided to use a patchwork as a wall hanging there is no need to use a layer of wadding. Add a series of evenly spaced loops across the top edge through which a hanging rod can be threaded.

Previous page 56: Often the simplest arrangement of squares is the most effective. Here, the thoughtful choice and arrangement of a few strong shades combined with the calming cream-colored fabric have produced eye-catching and attractive patterns.

Previous page 57: Quilts of this size and complexity really need machine stitching, although, of course, only a few generations ago they would have been worked by hand. Before you begin an ambitious project such as this, work out your pattern scheme on graph paper and, even though it sounds obvious, make sure that you buy enough fabric for all the pieces. Even if you manage to find the same pattern, dyes are not consistent, and it would be heart-breaking to embark on a set like this and to be unable to complete it with the same material.

Right: Finish off your bedroom with pillow case covers made with a pieced patch-work design that reflects the design of the quilt itself.

Opposite: Block patchwork quilts are comparatively quick to make. Use cream or white fabric to hold the overall design together, especially if you are using a patterned fabric for the larger pieces.

beautiful quilts that are now so well known and collected. Today, patchwork is no longer just a good way of using up scraps of materials or of extending the life of worn-out clothes – it is an art form in its own right.

Although patchwork is traditionally made from scraps of material of various weights, the best results are obtained from cottons of the same weight – 100 per cent cotton is ideal. Wash the material before you make it up. If nothing else, this will identify any colors that are not fast. You will also need a rotary cutter and mat. A rotary cutter may seem like a luxury, but when you are making a carefully planned patchwork, the pieces need to be accurately cut and a rotary cutter, which can cut through up to six layers of fabric at a time, will save you endless time. Even if you are not working a named pattern, it is worth using graph paper to chart the colors you intend to use and to plan the overall design.

Dating from about 1850 and made in Watertown, New York, this traditional friendship album patch quilt with signatures has a Flying Geese border. The quilt measures 68 x 87in (173 x 221cm).

Dating from about 1910, this Ocean Waves quilt from Pennsylvania measures 75 x 83in (191 x 211cm).

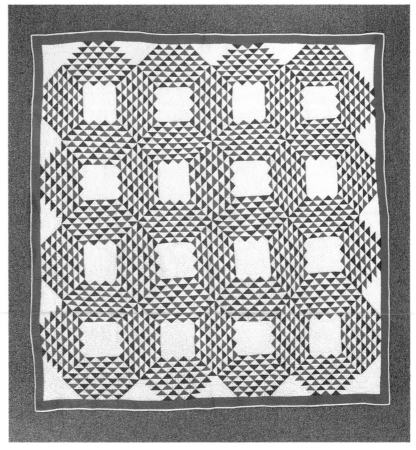

This unusual patchwork, which is 79 x 86in (201 x 218cm), was made in Illinois about 1910. The design is known as Wheels, and it was worked in wool.

If you do not want to buy a template, make your own hexagons with a pair of compasses. Honeycomb patterns are easily built up, but hexagons can also be used to make small rosettes of seven shapes, which are pieced together to make larger patterns, or they can be stitched together in rows to create interesting striped effects. You can also combine hexagons with diamonds and squares.

The subtle shades chosen for this Four Patch pieced quilt enhance the basically simple pattern. The patchwork, which was worked in wool, was made in New Mexico about 1940, and it measures 69 x 80in (175 x 203cm).

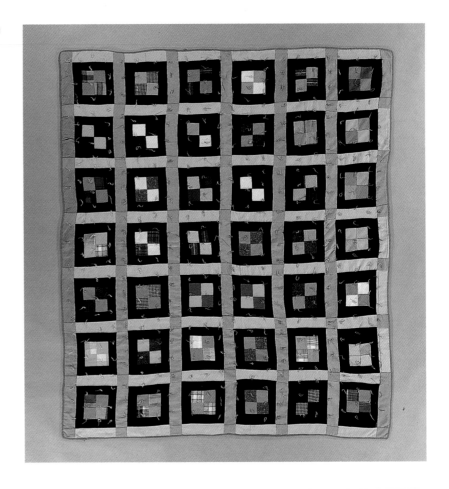

The central shape of this Star of Bethlehem patchwork was worked from small diamonds, while the outer border is formed from right-angled triangles. It was made from cotton about 1920 in Pennsylvania.

This pieced patchwork measures 70 x 72in (178 x 183cm). It was worked in wool and cotton in a design known as Fans, which was, in various forms, popular in the early half of the nineteenth century. This particular example, which was made in Pennsylvania, was completed about 1900.

This is an early example – made in Ohio about 1840 – of the famous pattern Tumbling Blocks. It was worked in cotton and measures 70 x 80in (178 x 203cm).

This detail from a pieced quilt measuring, overall, 81 x 82in (206 x 208cm), is a fine example of the Orange Peel design. It was worked in cotton about 1840, and was made in Ohio.

Choose your colors with care. Some of the most striking patchwork is made not with an accumulation of fabrics left over from every dress you have ever made, but with a carefully chosen balance of plain and patterned fabrics, and of light and dark tones. Part of the attraction of the wonderful Amish quilts lies in the glowing, clear colors that are used and the way in which they contrast with dark browns and blues or even black.

There are many named patterns. One of the earliest designs to be used in North America is known as Roman Squares. This consists of squares stitched from three strips. The squares are then stitched into long rows, with the direction of the three strips alternating. These long strips are stitched together and angled so that the direction of the three strips alternates to create an overall basketweave pattern. The corners are small triangles, and there are larger triangles around the edges to make a straight edge.

Ohio Star is pieced together from squares built up from nine squares. The nine small squares are themselves made up of five plain squares and four squares each made from four equilateral triangles. Careful cutting and seaming is essential so that the corners of the squares and triangles meet exactly.

One of the best known patterns is Log Cabin, which looks complicated but is, in fact, quite easy to stitch once you are quite confident about the order in which the pieces are added. A single square built up from the Log Cabin pattern makes an effective cushion cover, while several individual blocks can be stitched together to make a quilt.

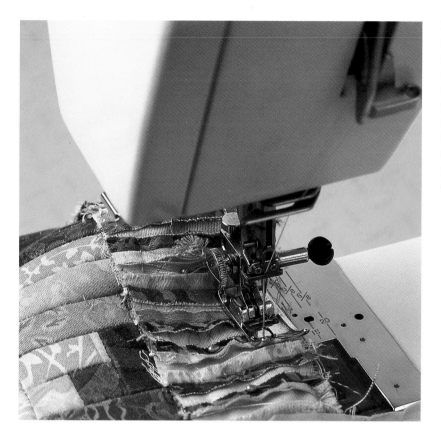

Log Cabin patchwork is best worked with a sewing machine. The cushion cover (illustrated overleaf) was made from six small motifs, pieced together and edged with a border made from strips of the materials used for the main motifs. Stitch strips together that are sufficiently long to be cut into the four widths you need to surround the completed cushion. Use pins to make sure that the raw edges do not get caught on the foot of your machine.

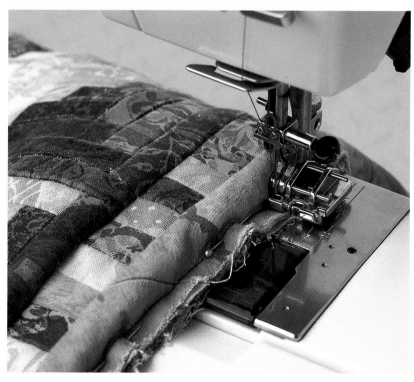

This cushion cover was finished off with a piping made from bias strips of one of the fabrics used for the patchwork pieces. Because Log Cabin is made from so many small pieces, it can look overly fussy if you try to introduce too many different shades.

Traditional English patchwork patterns often include hexagons, worked in patterns such as Grandmother's Flower Garden. Frame or medallion patterns, in which a central square or diamond, itself often made up of small pieces, is surrounded with symmetrical strips to form a square, were also popular in England. If you are working with hexagons you must use a card or plastic template.

Quilting

The oldest type of quilts were made from sandwiches of padding between two fabrics, which are then stitched together. The stitching serves two purposes — it holds the layers together but it is also decorative. Their original purpose was simply to provide warmth, whether in the form of clothing or bed covering, and all kinds of materials were used, including feathers, bits of old blankets and even bits of old clothes. Today, however, the padding is usually a light or medium weight polyester wadding, which is available in various widths, and some specialist shops supply wadding in widths suitable for a double-bed size quilt. The backing fabric should be good quality calico or a firm cotton such as sheeting.

The traditional wholecloth quilt — that is, one made from a piece or pieces of a plain fabric such as good quality cotton, densely woven silk or satin — is stitched with a thread that matches the fabric, although a contrasting color can look extremely attractive. Use a buttonhole twist thread — the best you can afford — which gives a firmer, clearer stitching line than ordinary sewing cotton. Plain fabric shows the stitched pattern much more clearly than patterned materials, but if you use patterned fabric, the stitch-

Opposite: Log Cabin pieces are often worked with a red square in the centre, and in North America this square represents the centre of the home — the hearth. Although it is so popular in the United States and its name is redolent of the pioneering life, the basic Log Cabin pattern originated in Britain. Here it has been used in a range of subtly contrasting shades to create a large cushion cover.

Left: As snug as a... This pretty but practical quilt has been made from easy-to-wash cotton and lightweight polyester wadding. Tiny white ribbon bows at the interstices of the squares are the perfect finishing touch.

ing can be done around motifs to highlight them and emphasize the design of the fabric. Quilting can be done by hand (you will need a frame), but it is much easier to stitch the long lines needed to outline shapes and the traditional patterns with a sewing machine.

The design must be marked on the top fabric before it is placed on the wadding and backing. Depending on the color and type of the fabric, use dressmaker's carbon paper, dressmaker's chalk or a blue water-erasable marker. A geometric repeating pattern can most easily be transferred if you make a template and simply draw round that.

If you have made a patchwork, it can be quilted in much the same way as a plain quilt, but you will need to follow the stitching line between groups of pieces.

Trapunto

An easy method of quilting, which is particularly useful for fairly small articles, is trapunto or stuffed quilting, in which selected areas of a piece of work are padded. The technique can be used with both pictorial and geometric designs. You need two layers of fabric – the top layer should be a closely woven silk or cotton and the lower layer should be a lighter, open-weave material or old sheeting. Transfer the design to the top fabric using a water-soluble pen. Place this piece on top of the backing fabric and pin then baste the two pieces together. Make sure that you use several vertical and horizontal rows of basting stitches so that the two pieces of material are held firmly together. If you are working by hand, use a small running stitch or back stitch to stitch along all the lines of the design. If you are using a machine, set it for a small straight stitch. When you have gone over all the lines of the design fasten off all loose ends securely.

Remove all basting stitches and turn over the work. Make a small slit in the backing fabric of any section of the work that is to be padded. Do this extremely carefully – you must not cut through the front fabric. Insert small amounts of polyester wadding through the slit. Do not use cotton wool, which goes lumpy, or sheets of wadding; you will get far better results if you use the kind of wadding that is sold loose for stuffing soft toys. Add it a pinch a time, using the blunt end of a knitting needle to push it into the shape. Check from the front that the wadding is smooth and fills the corners of the motif. When you are satisfied, close the slit with small overstitches.

Italian or corded quilting

This is a purely decorative technique that lends itself very well to linear designs. As with trapunto, you need two layers of fabric for Italian quilting – the top one should be a smooth, densely woven material and the backing fabric can be cotton with a loose, open weave or butter muslin. The design is achieved by stitching two close, parallel lines. The channel between the lines is then filled with quilting wool or soft cotton cord.

Transfer the design to the right side of the top fabric, using the prick and pounce method. Pin and baste the top fabric to the backing fabric, using vertical and horizontal lines. Use a matching thread and work in back stitch or small running stitch to stitch along the two lines of the design. Because

the cords cannot overlap, decide which lines will appear to go under and which will appear to go over each other. If the pattern is fairly straightforward, you can use a sewing machine. Fasten off all loose ends securely. Remove the basting stitches.

Turn over the piece and make an entry hole in the backing fabric. Be careful not to pierce the top layer. Thread the quilting wool or soft cord on to a bodkin and begin to thread it through the channel.

At corners or angles, bring the cord through the back and leave a small loop before reinserting the bodkin through the same hole but pointing in the new direction.

As in so many things, the simplest ideas are often the best. Colored cord has been threaded through parallel rows of stitching in this double layer of net curtaining to provide privacy with the maximum of light.

Right: You can use the basic technique for corded quilting without having a backing fabric. See pages 71–72.

Below: At its best, Italian quilting, in which cord is introduced into a narrow channel between two stitched lines, creates wonderfully decorative articles. The use of pink to stitch the lines of the petals and border enhances this simple pattern of stylized flowers and leaves.

Italian corded quilting is a time-consuming technique and is really suitable for objects such as cushion covers or even items such as belts, because the backing fabric needs to be covered. It is, however, possible to create the effect of corded quilting without a backing fabric.

1. Select a simple motif and use dressmaker's carbon to transfer it to the napkin.

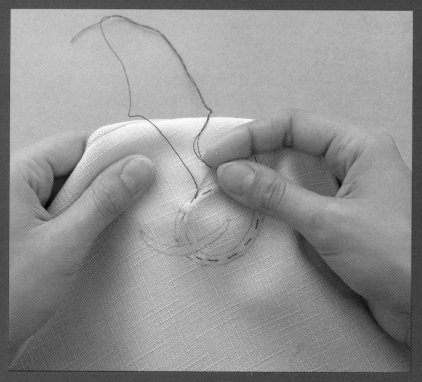

2. Baste the soft cotton cord to the shape of the motif. Try to keep your basting stitches in the centre of the two lines of the motif.

3. Use a contrasting color thread to stitch the cord in place. From the front it will look like two parallel rows of small back stitch.

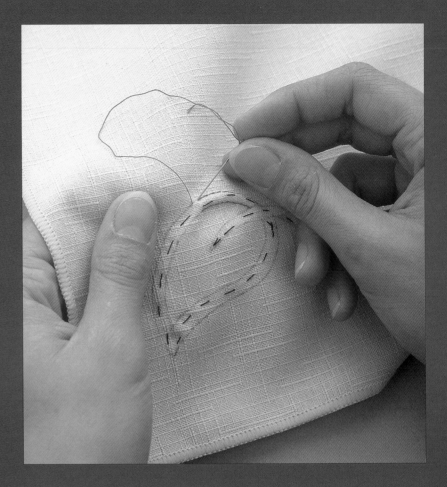

4. The cord is held in place by working stitches at alternate sides of the cord. Work from the front to make sure that your stitches are exactly on the drawn line and make sure that you do not stitch so tightly that the fabric puckers.

Appliqué

Appliqué is an easy way of combining the techniques of patchwork and quilting. The motifs you use can be as complicated or as simple as you wish, and it is the ideal way of disguising a hole or stain in any otherwise usable garment or piece of fabric. When the technique is used for articles such as table mats, a little lightweight padding can be inserted between the backing fabric and the cut-out shape.

You can use almost any fabric you wish, but check that they are all washable and pre-shrunk. Try to make sure that all the fabrics you use are a similar weight, and if you are working cushion covers or a bedspread, use a good, tightly woven cotton. Wall hangings and small decorative items can be worked with silk or satin, while velvet can look luxurious. You can also use ribbons and braids as trims and decorations.

At its simplest, you can appliqué a single motif to, say, a cushion cover. Apply iron-on interfacing to the wrong side of the fabric. Pinking shears are useful because they help prevent the fabric from fraying. If you are going to stitch by hand, allow a $1/4$in (5mm) turn in all round, snipping the fabric to the seam allowance so that it will lie flat when it is turned under; press down the seam allowance. If you are going to use a machine, cut on the line. Cut out the motif of your choice and pin and baste it to the background, making sure that there are no puckers on the underlying fabric. Stitch by hand with tiny slip stitches, making sure that the seam allowance

Previous page 73: This simple white cotton christening robe has been transformed by the addition of appliquéd flowers and leaves. Machine stitch the shapes in place, using a thread that closely matches the shade of the motifs.

This wonderful example of appliquéd tulips dates from 1854. It was made of cotton and comes from Alabama.

Opposite: Appliqué – is often used to decorate fairly small objects, but the technique has been used to create this colorful rug, which glows against the dark wooden floor.

This cheerful cushion cover has, unusually, a hessian base, on to which the appliqué pieces have been stitched. This is an excellent example of how even patterned fabric can be used to create strongly defined shapes.

go round. If you use a machine, use a close zigzag stitch, either in the same color as the motif or in a contrasting shade.

More complicated motifs can be applied in the same way, and the technique is especially suitable for pictorial motifs. Back all the fabrics you need with iron-on interfacing, but leave the backing sheet in place for the time being. Plan your design carefully and copy it on to tracing paper; keep this copy for reference. Make a second tracing of your design, but this time mark on it the overlaps and any stitching lines. Cut up the tracing and use the pieces as templates to cut out your fabric pieces. Assemble the pieces on the backing fabric, using your first tracing as reference. Stitch around the shapes as before.

Appliqué perse – Persian appliqué – is the technique by which motifs from printed fabrics are cut out and applied to a plain background. It is a useful way of using up off cuts of furnishing fabrics, which should be washed to check for shrinking and color fastness before they are used. Cut out a motif or several motifs and arrange them on the backing fabric until you are happy with the arrangement, then pin and baste in place. Attach with a close zigzag machine stitch or buttonhole all round if you are stitching by hand.

Opposite: At first glance this looks like a piece of stained glass, but closer inspection reveals that it is, in fact, an appliquéd design, with narrow strips of black bias-cut fabric used to represent the lead cames that hold pieces of glass in place.

This charming family of mice has been appliquéd to a plain cotton base. Modern lightweight cottons are color fast and washable and are ideal for quilts such as this. Don't forget to add eyes and mouths to your mice, and use the close zigzag setting on your machine to create a smooth, defining edge around each shape.

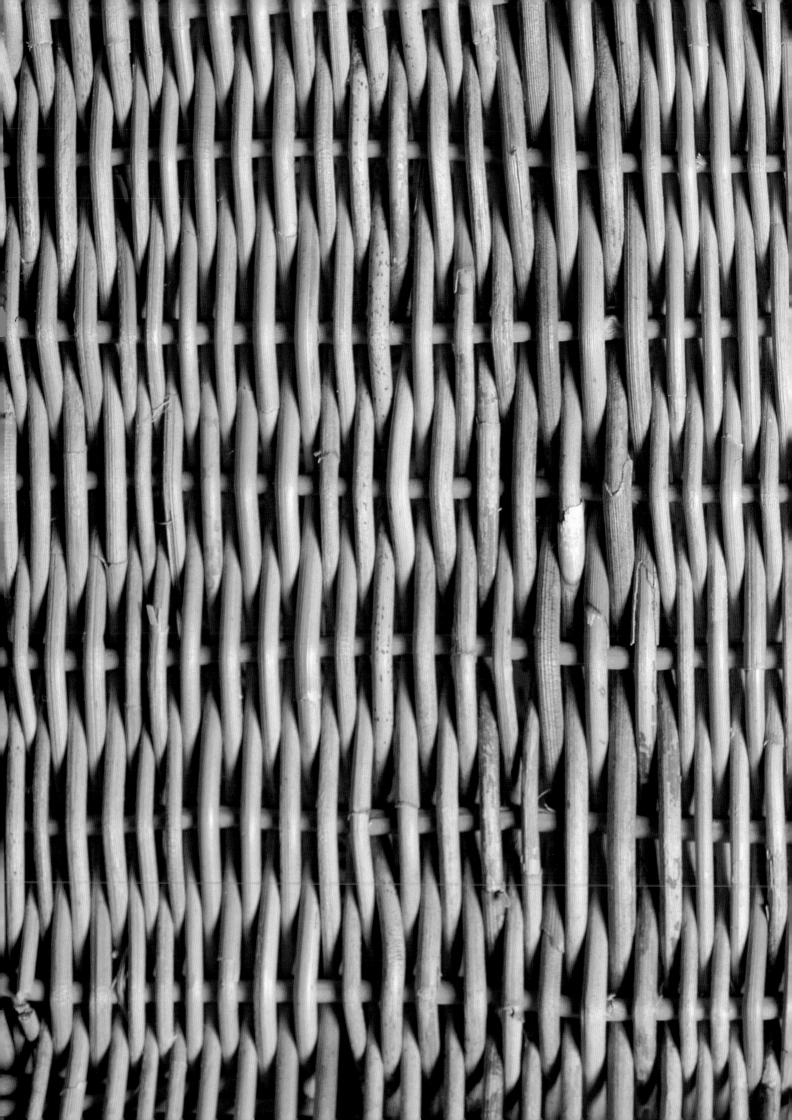

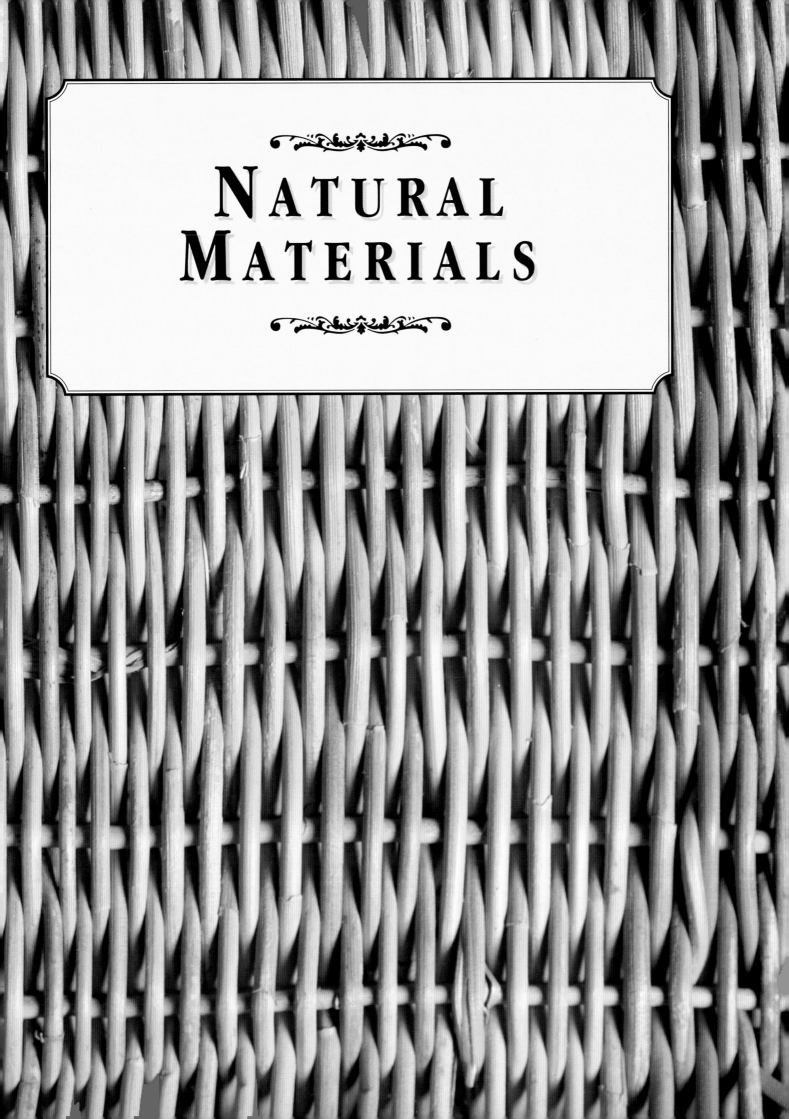

NATURAL
MATERIALS

The desire to repair or restore an old chair or basket may encourage you to try caning and rushwork, crafts that have scarcely changed for centuries. Using these natural materials is a wonderful way of giving a new lease of life to a battered basket or sagging chair, but once you have mastered the basic skills, you will want to create entirely new articles. The traditional methods can be easily adapted to modern styles, while old pictures often include old-fashioned baskets and chair seats that will give you ideas for your own designs.

Baskets and Basketry

One of the most attractive of all the traditional crafts, basketry offers the home worker the most satisfying range of materials – willow, rush, raffia, straw, cane as well as specially grown coppice woods and even palms – which can be used in a range of techniques that makes it possible to create an enormous variety of objects, from tiny egg cups to baskets and huge containers for pot plants.

There are five basic techniques, and they have been traditionally used to make specific objects and shapes. In Africa coiled baskets have been made for thousands of years. Natural and dyed leaves are stitched over a coil made of the rigid central ribs of the leaves to make mats, bowls, plates and baskets. In wickering or stake-and-strand, the base and sides are made of a framework of radiating rigid sticks (or, in rectangular or square baskets,

Opposite: It is hard to believe that the seat and back of this lovely chair were once torn and broken. Repairs to antique chairs can be made to look authentic by a careful choice of materials, which can be stained or dyed to a sympathetic shade.

Above: Beginning with a manageable project such as a basket is one of the best introductions to the craft.

Left: Although the tools required for basketwork are few, and most can be improvised, you need to work where you have plenty of space around you, and you may even choose to work outdoors. Remember, too, that rush and willow must be damp before you can work with them, so your working area must be large enough to accommodate a tub or trough of water.

parallel stick), interwoven with a pliable material. Willow and cane are usually used. Frame or ribbed baskets are worked on a rigid hoop-shaped frame, and the ribs are added as work progresses. The technique differs mainly from wickering because the weaving is done from the edge downwards, while in wickering the sides of the basket are built up from the base. Plaited mats and baskets are made from flexible materials such as palm, rushes and grasses, and similar pliable materials are used for both the uprights and weavers of twined objects.

In addition to the traditional methods and materials, there are dozens of different finishes and ways of shaping the object or of adding handles. You will also need special tools, including bodkins, pliers, bradawls, a rapping iron (for tapping down the woven rows) and secateurs.

Most home basket work is done with cane or willow. The cane used for basket making is available in about 15 different sizes from large craft shops. It has to be soaked in warm water for 15–20 minutes before use so that it is supple enough to work with. Some craft shops also stock willow, which is shinier and thicker than cane.

Because there are so many possible combinations of technique and materials, you might want to consider attending evening classes to gain an understanding of the different effects that can be achieved with the huge range of materials that are available.

Opposite: Wooden bases for trays and baskets are available in most craft shops. These bases used to be made of birch or oak, but now you are more likely to find plywood or even plastic.

Project
Tray and Glass Holders

You can buy wooden bases with ready-drilled holes in them as well as suitable staves in most craft shops. The bottom ends of the basket staves are woven beneath the base to create a foot-border that is known as a trac.

1. Thread the staves through the pre-drilled holes in the base. You will need about 3in (7.5cm) of each stave to work the foot-border. Several different patterns can be worked, but a useful basic technique is behind one, in front of two, or simply, behind one, in front of one.

2. Weave the border. Again, there are numerous patterns and arrangements to choose from, but on a tray such as this, where the border is not deep, use a simple, regular weave.

3. The top border is worked with the standing staves. A simple border, in which the stave is simply passed before one, behind one, requires about 2in (5cm) of stave. More complicated plaited borders will need 9–10in (23– 25cm) of stave.

Rush is the ideal material for chair seats – it is soft and pliable – and in Britain by the early eighteenth century making rush-seated chairs was a flourishing home industry, with the menfolk making the frames while the women worked on the seats. Sadly, as these chairs reveal only too clearly, rush has a limited life. Restoring such chairs, however, is not beyond the scope of a careful homeworker.

This bow-fronted chair has been lovingly restored with a new cane seat. There are dozens of possible patterns to choose from, and there is nothing to stop you from selecting any style that you particularly like. Often, however, it is interesting to try to reproduce the original pattern, which you may be able to discern in any small patches of the seating that remain.

Wreaths

Many craft shops and flower shops stock wire and floral foam wreaths into which fresh flowers and sprigs of foliage can be inserted. However, unless you use dried plant material or unless you have chosen your plants so that they can be allowed to dry out naturally while retaining their color and form, such arrangements have only a limited life.

Look out for rings that are made of a woody material such as straw, vine stems or raffia. Some shops also stock willow and wicker rings, which are attractive in their own right and can be hung up as they are or simply decorated with a ribbon. A quick, attractive and useful way of using a natural

Basket and wickerwork are especially appropriate for conservatories and summerhouses. If you plan to use these materials outdoors, apply coats of polyurethane varnish to protect them from sudden showers.

ring, however, is to use it to make a herb ring for your kitchen. As they dry many herbs tend to become rather brittle, and it is often easier to work with small bunches of freshly picked herbs that can be allowed to dry out in situ. Pick little sprigs of strongly scented herbs, such as bay, rosemary, thyme, sweet marjoram and, of course, mint, and wire each type of herb in little bunches with medium stubb wires. Attach the herbs to the ring, attaching them so that they lie at an angle. If you like the appearance of the underlying ring, tie in the herbs carefully so that the stubb wires cannot be seen, or add so many little bunches that the underlying ring is completely hidden.

A natural looking basket the color of corn that will add a special detail to any kitchen or living area.

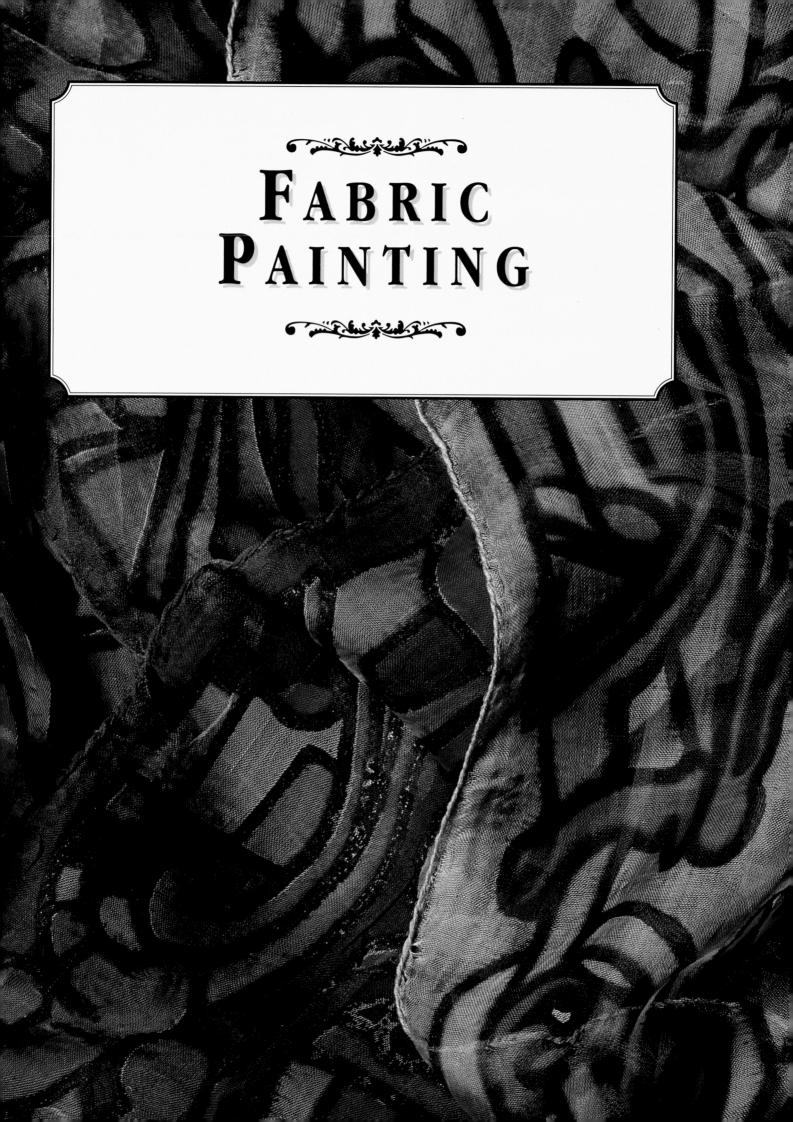

FABRIC
PAINTING

There may be occasions when you want to decorate a piece of fabric but do not want to embroider or decorate it with stitching. Fabric paints and dyes now make it easy to change or add colors. Remember that natural fabrics, such as cotton, respond best because they absorb the color. Fabrics such glazed chintz, on the other hand, do not always work as well because the color tends to sit on the surface of the fibres.

Cold water dyes, which are specially designed for hand dyeing in cold water, can be used to color natural fibres – cotton, linen, silks and lighter colors of wool – permanently and easily. These paints can also be used with tie-dye and batik techniques. Tie-dye involves folding, pleating, knotting or otherwise fastening a fabric to prevent the dye from reaching all areas of a fabric. Batik is a method of creating pattern on fabric by using a wax resist. Both techniques can be used to make curtains and hangings and, with practice, they can be used to create sophisticated and complex patterns. Batik, in particular, can be used for multicolored designs, but remember that each color requires a new application of the resist.

Far easier to apply are the ordinary fabric paints, which can be applied straight from the bottle or mixed in a palette and applied with a paintbrush to decorate all types of cotton. If you are artistic, use the paints and pens to draw freehand patterns. If you prefer, the same paints can be used with masking and stencilling to create repeating patterns and motifs. Stencilled patterns are especially appropriate for bed and table linen, and using this technique will enable you to decorate, say, a bedspread or duvet cover by picking out a motif or color from your wallpaper or curtains.

Of all the natural fibres, silk is the most luxurious and in many ways one of the most rewarding of all materials to work with. Silk for scarves can be bought with ready-rolled edges, and if you are planning to make a scarf for yourself or as a gift, buy one that is already hemmed: life is too short to roll and hem all four sides of large silk square.

When it comes to furnishing or dress-making, however, you need to buy silk by the yard or metre. Your local needlecraft shop or even the haberdashery department of a large department store may not stock a wide selection of silks, but it is worth persevering to find a weight and weave that you like and that is appropriate to your needs. A cushion cover, for example, will need a fairly robust silk such as heavyweight habutai. Look out, too, for twill, a type of silk with a distinctive diagonal weave.

Paints for silk are of two main kinds – those that are fixed by steaming and those that can be fixed by ironing. Some people claim that the colors achieved by steam-fixing are superior to those that can be obtain with iron-fixed paints because the colors are absorbed into the fibres of the silk rather than simply resting on top. The drawback to steam-fixed paints is that the process usually has to be done commercially, and although specialist silk and silk paint suppliers can often recommend companies that can help, this does add to the cost of the process. If you are feeling adventurous and have been working on a fairly small piece, you can steam-fix in a pressure cooker. Iron the paints when they are dry, place the fabric on kitchen paper, then cover it with more kitchen paper. You must make sure that areas of the silk cannot come into contact with each other or the paints

Opposite: Using a resist such as gutta to draw your design on a piece of silk allows you to paint precise patterns in contrasting colors. You must stretch the silk on a frame if you use gutta, or the paints will run and smudge.

95

will smudge and spoil. Roll up the paper and silk sandwich and make a small parcel, wrapped in aluminium foil. Steam the package, suspended in a basket above about 3in (7.5cm) of water, for approximately 45 minutes.

Iron-fixed paints, on the other hand, are simply ironed for 2–3 minutes on the reverse with a warm iron (do not use your steam setting) when the paint is dry. Protect your ironing board with a spare piece of cotton. The colors are then fast, washable – to about 140°F (60°C) – and dry cleanable. There are up to 50 shades, which can be mixed together or with a proprietary diluent or a mixing white to make new shades.

There is also a range of paints in the form of pens, which are easy to apply, and are ideal for outline patterns or writing. These pen-paints are fixed by dry ironing on the reverse or under a cloth, and the colors can be washed about a day after iron fixing. At present there are 18 colors (including six bright fluorescent shades), and no doubt new shades will be available before long.

Iron-fixed paints can also be heat-set by wrapping them in aluminium foil and placing them in the oven, pre-heated to about 300°F (150°C), for 10–15 minutes. You can also use your microwave oven to heat set silk paints, but wrap the silk in kitchen paper, not foil.

Some of the loveliest effects are achieved by applying the silk paints wet on wet. Thin the paints with water if you wish or mix two colors in a palette, and use a broad paintbrush or, for really large areas, a sponge, to apply one color. Then, before the first color dries, apply a second color, allowing them to mix as they abut. The two shades will merge together to create new, subtle shades. When you apply one color on top of another you will create new, iridescent tones.

Experiment by sprinkling salt on the still wet paints. As the salt absorbs the paint, it creates interesting star-burst effects. Apply a strong solution of sugar and water and use a pipette to drop the solution on to the wet paint. As it dries, you will get a wonderful impression of flowers. Fold the fabric, concertina-style, and drop paint on it so that the color penetrates to different depths to create unusual stripes.

Although silk paints can be used in a host of ways to produce subtly shaded abstract patterns, they can also be used for detailed, precise designs. This involves the use of gutta or resist, and when you work with gutta you will also need to stretch the silk on a frame. You can buy purpose-made frames, some of the more sophisticated kinds being adjustable to suit a range of sizes. If you do not want to buy a special frame, use an old picture frame or, if you are working on a fairly small piece, use an embroidery hoop, binding the rings with masking tape to protect the fabric. If you do pin the silk to a wooden frame, use special three-pronged pins. Drawing pins will leave a hole in the silk. Stretch the fabric across the frame, placing the pins at intervals on opposite sides, then inserting more pins until the silk is stretched taut in the frame. Try to avoid placing the pins immediately opposite each other, which tends to cause ridges in the silk.

You can buy spirit-based and water-based gutta, but if you are using iron-fixed paints, use water-based gutta, which will wash out when the paints have been fixed. The gutta is applied from a bottle with a nozzle in the top. For exceptionally fine lines, a nib can be inserted in the nozzle. Hold the

gutta bottle almost vertical so that the gutta flows out smoothly and evenly. You must take care that there are no gaps or breaks in the line you draw, because the paints will flow through the lines. The gutta must penetrate the silk fibres, rather than simply resting in a line on the top of the fabric. Allow the gutta to dry, then apply the silk paint, using a brush to place it in the centre of the outlined area and to guide it towards the gutta line. Allow one color to dry before applying the next.

The great beauty of working with silk is that you do not have to be a good artist to produce some really lovely work. You can copy a design you like, enlarging it on a photocopier or by the grid method if necessary, and go over the lines with a black pen. Use masking tape to hold the design under the silk in the frame or, if it does not matter if the pattern is reversed, turn over the frame so that the silk rests on the design. Go over the outlines with gutta. Use a fabric marker to trace the design, turn over the frame or remove the redrawn design, then go over the lines with gutta and use silk paints as before.

The finest of lightweight silks have an indefinable quality that enhances the appearance of the paints you use and makes silk one of the most rewarding of materials to work with. Sturdier and heavier silks are surprisingly hard wearing, and there is no reason you cannot use them for cushion covers and soft furnishings.

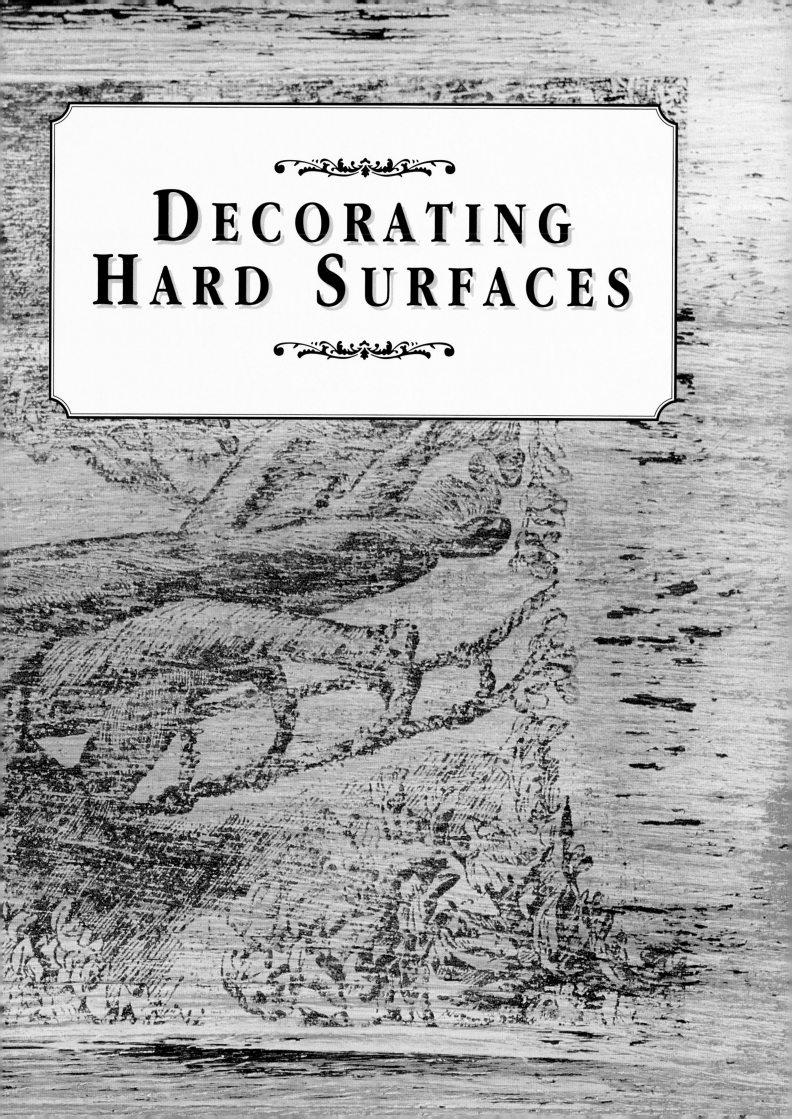

DECORATING
HARD SURFACES

Opposite: A plain wooden tray has been transformed by a simple stencil and the use of a single color. Transparent acetate stencils have the great advantage that they allow you to position them precisely, without the guesswork involved in using opaque stencils.

The revival in interest in using paints to add decorative details rather than simply providing a background color has made such techniques as stencilling, stippling, spattering, ragging, marbling, feathering and sponging familiar to us all. However, rather than simply use these to decorate walls, think about using the same techniques on wooden furniture (including wicker) and smaller decorative objects. Pelmets and doors can also be painted to transform the appearance of a room. The great advantage of paint that it can always be covered by an another coat if you do not like the end result or, if the worst comes to the worst, it can be removed completely.

Brighten up a child's bedroom with this attractive wall hanging, which was made to protect the painted wall behind a table on which there was a railway layout. The shape was cut from plywood, although MDF (medium density fiberboard) would be a good alternative, and the rough edges were thoroughly sanded and smoothed before the surface was primed and prepared for painting. The design was carefully planned on rough paper before being transferred to the surface of the wood, and the finished work was given several coats of clear polyurethane varnish to protect it.

Although you can buy a variety of pretty stencils, ready cut out for use, think about making your own design based on, say, a motif in your furnishing fabrics. The outlines are simplified and stylized, so you do not have to have a high level of artistic skill, and some old patterns have recently been republished so you can photocopy and enlarge or reduce a motif to suit the scale of your room. Use special stencil paper (which does not tear easily) or tough acetate film.

Stencilling does not have to be used only on your walls – think about floors, ceilings, furnishings and fabrics – and when you want a change, you can simply paint over it and begin again.

Sponging off is a useful technique if you want a delicate appearance of depth. Apply a base coat of silk emulsion (latex) paint (we used cream) and leave it to dry before applying the glaze coat of the second color.

Work quickly with your sponge before the second coat dries. As you apply the sponge to the wall, vary the pattern by turning your hand slightly each time, and occasionally change the position of the sponge in your hand. Because the second coat has to be sponged off before it dries, you should work on a small area at a time – or get a friend to help.

Painting on Wood

One of the best ways of reviving an old and perhaps treasured piece of wooden furniture or even a picture or mirror frame is to disguise its imperfections with stencilling.

Whether you are working on a chest of drawers or a tray, you must strip off all the old paint, varnish, polish or wax and fill any cracks. Preparing the surface thoroughly will make all the difference to the end result. White spirit will remove dirt and polish and most kinds of wax and oil-based finishes. Methylated spirits will be needed to remove shellac and most old varnishes. A proprietary paint stripper especially designed for furniture can be used to remove cellulose-based varnishes.

Take care that you do not raise the grain of the wood, but you may need to rub down the surface. Use several grades of sandpaper, working from coarse to fine, and always in the direction of the grain. Use a knotting compound on any knots that have been revealed. If you want a natural wood, use a stain, applying it thinly with a dry brush.

Above: This tin tray, which was painted in Sweden about 1920, is almost too pretty to use. If you find an old metal tray, carefully remove all traces of rust with a proprietary remover (you will find this in a motor accessory shop) and apply a coat of special rust-retardant paint before you begin to think about decorating it. If you do not think your artistic skills are up to producing anything as delicate as this, you might want to think about découpage.

Opposite: "On the second day of Christmas, my true love sent to me, two turtle doves" – and this charming illustration has been painted on the front of a small pine cupboard. You must remove all existing paint and varnish and prime the wood before you begin.

Salt is one of the commodities that everyone has in the kitchen but that is usually sold in rather unattractive containers. This old wooden box was transformed by careful stripping, rubbing down and priming before the painted decoration was added. The salt itself is kept in a glass jar inside the box.

The bleached, limed look can be achieved by scouring the surface of the wood once you have removed all the old paint, varnish, wax and so on. Use steel wool and a wire brush to open the grain, then rub white emulsion paint into the grain. Tint the white paint with gray or the palest blue, allow to dry then apply the stencilled decoration. If you wish and if the object is likely to be subject to a certain amount of wear, finish with a coat of polyurethane, preferably with a matt finish.

Découpage

This is the ideal technique for those whose artistic ambitions outstrip their artistic skills. Découpage – the word derives from the French *decouper*, to cut out – is the art of using designs and cut out shapes to decorate anything from a simple box to lampshades, trays and even quite large pieces of furniture.

Screens are little used these days, but they can be useful – especially in a large, drafty room. They can also be used to provide a kind of large-scale photograph album. Battered screens occasionally turn up in auctions and second-hand furniture shops, but if you have access to a well-equipped workshop or know a well-disposed timber merchant, you might want to consider making a simple three-panelled screen from MDF or plywood. Hinge the panels so that the screen folds into a Z-shape – it will not stand upright if you do not. Prepare and prime the surface, then decorate it with cut-outs of your choice. We used flower motifs from wallpaper. The aim of découpage is to make the edges of the cut-out images disappear in the layers of varnish that are applied – so make sure you like the arrangement before you begin.

Natural sponges should always be used for sponging. Synthetic sponges, although cheap and widely available, do not produce the delightfully random effect of a natural sponge. If you really cannot find a natural sponge – and the upsurge in interest in textured paint effects means that they can now be found in paint stores as well as health food shops – tear a dry, synthetic household sponge to create a jagged surface.

The technique is believed to have originated in Venice in the seventeenth century, and it is known in Italy as the poor man's art, *art del povera* or *arte povero*. It arose because Italian furniture makers were striving to find some way of simulating the extravagantly decorated and lacquered furniture that was being imported into Europe from China and Japan. The decorations were covered with many layers of protective lacquer, and in Britain the technique became known as Japanning. The style spread throughout Europe, with national styles developing as the eighteenth century progressed. In France, for example, delicate flowers, *putti* and pretty motifs were used, and engravings by such artists as François Boucher, Jean-Baptiste Pillement and Jean-Antoine Watteau were widely used. In 1762 the London publisher and print-seller Robert Sayer produced the first edition of a book entitled *The Ladies Amusement or Whole Art of Japanning Made Easy*, which was an enormously popular compendium of rococo designs, including many by Pillement and other French artists and also by the English artist Thomas Bewick and the German designers Johann George Hertel and Martin Engelbrecht, who engraved and published rococo and chinoiserie designs.

In Victorian Britain the technique achieved new heights, with three-dimensional, embossed designs created from hand-colored motifs cut out from specially published scrap books. This high degree of ornamentation was paralleled in Germany, where the technique was often used to decorate Biedermeier furniture. Although découpage was so popular in Victorian Britain that it was used on almost anything that had a flat surface, in many ways the technique was debased. Instead of cutting out many small motifs and illustrations and building them up into a new design or pattern, the tendency was simply to cut out entire scenes or illustrations and paste them in position.

Today, découpage is enjoying something of a revival again, and new materials and design ideas can be happily combined with the old idea to decorate an enormous range of articles from furniture and small, everyday articles, and it is used on a wide range of materials, ranging from wood to glass, tin, china, glass and even plastic. Provided that you prepare the surface properly, découpage can be used on practically anything.

The first essential is to collect suitable illustrations. Gift wrapping paper, greeting cards, magazines and calendars offer a limitless variety of colorful images and motifs that can be cut out and collected. You should also look in newspapers and books for illustrations that can be photocopied and colored by hand. A photocopier is useful not only because it will allow you to make more than one copy of an image but also because you can enlarge or, more likely, reduce the motifs so that they are in proportion to the article that is to be decorated. Copy onto the finest paper available. As you become more interested in découpage you will find that you become aware of other, perhaps surprising sources of material – wallpaper, advertisements, packaging, stamps and even postcards.

In order to color the image or motif you will need to use oil-based crayons. Water-based crayons will run when they get wet, they do not give such good depth of color and the colors are, in any case, more fugitive than those resulting from oil-based pencils. Seal the print when you have colored it to prevent it from smearing and smudging while you glue and varnish it.

Opposite: This screen has been simply decorated with wallpaper to create a colorful focal point in an otherwise dark corner. There is no need to varnish the surface of single, large sheets of paper used in this way – regard a screen such as this, if you like, in the same way as your cushions and re-cover it when you decorate your room or change your curtains.

Metal surfaces lend themselves very well to découpage. This metal tray had seen better days and had one or two patches of rust, which were treated with a proprietary remover before the entire tray was painted with a coat of red oxide, rust-retardant paint and then ordinary black paint. The flowers were photocopied from a nine-teenth-century book and carefully hand-tinted before being cut out and arranged in the centre. The border was stencilled on with gold acrylic, and the entire tray was given several coats of matt varnish.

Opposite: We used shells to decorate this plain, wood-framed mirror, which provides a happy reminder of a sea-side holiday every morning.

Failing to prepare the surface properly is perhaps the single most common cause of failure. All surfaces must be thoroughly prepared and cleaned. Wood must be sanded down carefully, using at least two grades of sandpaper, before any cracks or gaps are filled. Gesso can be used to fill surface cracks and seal the grain of raw wood. Sand again then stain or paint before applying a sealer. Varnished or painted wood may need simply a light sanding before a sealant is applied or if the existing surface is in a poor condition you may have to remove the varnish or paint completely before sanding and re-painting. The main problem with metal surfaces is that they are prone to rust. Sand lightly and make sure you remove all traces of the dust before applying a metal primer. Other surfaces must be free from dust and grease before a clear sealer is applied.

The images can be cut out with tiny, sharp-pointed scissors or with a scalpel or the very point of a craft knife (work on a cutting mat if this is your preferred tool). Remember that you should not simply cut around the edge of the image but also remove any areas inside the illustration that are part of the background. Use a water-soluble paste – some craft shops now stock a special paste that is suitable for découpage – or use thinned PVA adhesive. You will find tweezers useful for holding and positioning small motifs, and you will also need a burnisher (the back of a small spoon will serve) to make sure that the image adheres completely to the surface. Work with a supply of paper towels or a clean cloth so that you can wipe away any smears of paste that appear as you press the image on to the background. Allow to dry for at least 24 hours before the next stage.

When it comes to applying the varnish you must work in a dry, dust-free and well-ventilated room. Although shellac was the favoured varnishing among Victorians and it is still used, it does tend to yellow with age. Unless you especially like shellac, use a clear varnish, which can be thinned with turpentine and cleaned away with paint remover. (If you have decorated an object made of plastic, remember that turpentine cannot be used on plastic.) Some writers suggest that you should apply up to 10 coats of varnish, and although you may find that four or five are ample, this is, nevertheless, a stage that cannot be hurried because each coat must be allowed to dry completely before the next is applied. When each coat is dry it should be lightly sanded to remove any specks of dust that are trapped in it. Do not attempt to rub down the surface before the varnish is absolutely dry, and to be on the safe side you need to allow a day between each coat. If you try to speed the process up by using a hair-drier or placing the object near a radiator the varnish will bubble or turn cloudy.

Shell Mirror

If you live near the coast or if you want to have happy memories of a holiday by the sea, use your collection of shells in a kind of three-dimensional découpage. As with all forms of decorating on wood, you must prepare the surface before you begin.

Once you have removed the old paint or varnish from an old mirror or picture frame, check that the corners are secure. Use a good wood glue in the corners. Holes can be filled by mixing sawdust with a little wood adhesive and using it instead of plastic wood. Rub down the surface, using

several grades of sand paper, then stain (if part of the frame is going to be visible under the decoration) and seal.

Before you attach anything to the frame, draw the outline on a clean sheet of paper and arrange on it the objects you are going to use. It is worth spending some time getting the design right now, and there is always the danger that if you begin to glue the decoration in place you will not have enough to complete the design. Use a fairly strong adhesive to stick the shells into position, and if the frame has an uneven profile it may be simpler to mix a small amount of interior wall filler to press the shells into so that they have a firm surface to adhere to.

Terracotta and Tiles

Ceramic tiles are ideal for decorating with stencils, and this is the perfect way of reviving your kitchen or bathroom without going to the expense of having the existing tiles removed and replaced.

If your kitchen or bathroom is decorated with plain tiles, rather than go to the expense of re-tiling, use a simple stencil to give the tiles a completely new look. In a room such as a kitchen or bathroom, where the tiles are liable to become wet through condensation or steam, you must use a good acrylic paint and protect the finished motifs with polyurethane or sealant.

Clean the surface thoroughly. It must be absolutely clean and grease-free. Remove as much grout as you can. Gloss ceramic tiles should be given an undercoat of eggshell emulsion before decorating. Because no surface decoration will be permanent on glazed ceramic unless it is fired into the ceramic, use a ceramic paint or acrylic for your stencilled design and seal it with polyurethane or a ceramic sealant.

Do not confine your paint techniques to indoors. All the basic methods can be applied to objects such as ceramic or terracotta pots. Make sure that the pot is clean and dry, then apply a coat of acrylic primer or gesso. When the primer is dry, apply the decoration of your choice in acrylic paint. The pattern can be as simple or as complex as you wish, although if you want a pictorial or geometric pattern you will need to plan it carefully to allow for the angle of the pot.

Finish with at least two coats of matt varnish, which should be applied both inside and outside to protect the design and make it waterproof.

Acrylic paint is so versatile that it can even be used on terracotta pots. You must seal the decorated pots inside and out to protect the paint from water.

MODELLING

Most of us will remember the satisfaction and enjoyment of using plasticine or modelling clay when we were children to make misshapen objects — animals that would not stand up and containers that would not lie down. Perhaps it is an atavistic gratification, but there are few more pleasing activities than using one's hands to turn an unprepossessing raw material into something attractive or useful. The last three crafts in this book use three totally dissimilar materials — papier mâché, paraffin wax and salt dough — to do just that. Working with papier mâché has a long and proud history, while salt dough is a more recent discovery. Both, however, offer real scope for self-expression and creativity at a fraction of the cost of many home crafts, while candle making is an absorbing and satisfying way of spending a rainy afternoon.

Papier Mâché

The making and use of papier mâché has a long history. It first appeared in France — the name is French for "chewed paper" — in the seventeenth century, but it really came into its own in the eighteenth century, when it was used to decorate stucco and plaster ceilings. As the name suggests, it is basically a paper pulp, mixed with a coloring agent (chalk was traditionally used) and an adhesive. Alternatively, strips of paper are glued together with a suitable paste and pressed into or around a mold or former.

In the eighteenth century Henry Cole of Birmingham, UK, developed a system of building up layers of paper, which were pressed into wooden molds. He used his method to make trays, screens and even furniture, and the objects he made in this way were carefully smoothed and varnished, often with black, green or crimson, to imitate the fashionable wares from Japan that were being imported at the time. Cole was so successful that he was appointed Japanner-in-Ordinary to George III and the Prince of Wales.

Nowadays we would hardly consider making furniture from papier mâché, although when it is properly made it is surprisingly strong. It can, however, be used to make a variety of household objects. In recent years papier mâché has gained a rather unfortunate reputation, chiefly because it is so easily made by children that it tends to be used for large, brightly colored objects such as masks. However, when it is carefully and precisely used, papier mâché offers considerable scope for imaginative projects. It is also one of the most satisfying of crafts, for although the technique is so simple, the results can be impressive.

Both the techniques — strips of paper and paper pulp — can be used. Both are inexpensive and both are easy to work with. The paste you use is a matter of personal preference, although few of us will choose to mix the flour and water paste that was traditionally used. Wallpaper paste is ideal. Not only is it comparatively inexpensive, but you can keep left-over paste in a tightly sealed container. Newsprint is often used, but it is indisputably dirty. In any case, when you are applying strips of paper in layers, it is useful to be able to see how far you have got to when you are applying a new layer, and one of the easiest ways of checking exactly where you are is to use different colors. The lighter and smoother the paper, the better the appearance of the finished object. Tear the strips — cutting them will create unwanted hard lines — and try to keep the pieces evenly sized. Mix the paste in a large bowl and dunk the strip right in it, squeezing it through your fingers to remove the excess paste, before you apply it. Papier mâché pulp is made by soaking small pieces of paper in water, squeezing them until they are almost dry and then mixing the pellets with paste. Again, the finer and lighter the paper you use, the better the appearance of the finished object.

One of the easiest ways of using the technique is to stick pieces of paper to a paper plate or dish, which is then left inside the finished object. Use fairly long strips, and apply several even layers, allowing the paste to dry thoroughly before you apply the next layer. Trim the edge with sharp scissors if necessary. Apply a coat of white primer and then decorate with poster or acrylic paints before varnishing.

Project
Papier Mâché Plate

One of the easiest ways to make a papier mâché plate is to use a sturdy paper plate — the kind you can buy in supermarkets for barbecues and picnics — and to use it as a former, leaving it inside the layers of pasted paper. More traditional, however, is to use a mold that is removed when the layers of paper have been allowed to dry.

1. Lightly grease the upper surface of your plate, making sure you do not use too much. Petroleum jelly is ideal, but you could brush on a little vegetable oil if you prefer.

2. Tear paper or newspaper into strips about 1in (2.5cm) wide and about 2in (5cm) longer than the diameter of the plate. Mix the wallpaper paste or, if you prefer, watered down PVA adhesive, and soak the first strips, which should be laid in the same direction across the plate until you have completely covered the surface of the plate. Press the paper down carefully into the dip of the bowl.

3. Lay the second layer of strips in the opposite direction to the first. This is when it is helpful to use colored paper so that you can see exactly which areas have been covered. You will need to apply about eight layers of paper strips in all, alternating the direction of each one so that the finished plate is really strong. When you have pasted the last layer down, leave the plate to dry, which can take up to 48 hours. Do not be tempted to try to hurry this process along by leaving the plate on a radiator or in sunshine, or you may cause the papier mache to warp or buckle.

4. When the papier mâché is dry, use sharp scissors to trim away the excess around the edge, then insert the end of a knife between the plate and the papier mache . The plate should come away easily. To create a neat, strong edge, apply a row of pasted paper strips right around the circumference, so that the trimmed raw edge is completely covered. Leave the plate in a warm, airy place until it is absolutely dry.

5. Rub down the surface very lightly with fine sandpaper, then apply at least two coats of white primer. When the paint is dry, check for any rough areas and rub down gently. Use the white primer to touch up any areas that you have rubbed down, then your plate is ready for decorating.

You can decorate papier mâché in any way you like. The undercoat will accept acrylic paints or you can use brightly colored poster paints. Remember to apply at least two coats of clear varnish when you have finished to protect the surface – and don't forget the back.

More challenging is to make a box. If you do not have a suitably sized cardboard box, cut six pieces of lightweight card, measuring them carefully so that the base, sides and top fit accurately together. Use strips of pasted paper or masking tape to hold the base to the sides and also the sides to the adjacent sides. Cover the base and sides, inside and out, with a layer of paper strips, covering the joins carefully, and apply a layer of strips to the top. Allow to dry, then use masking tape to create a hinge to join the top to one side. Apply another layer to the box, inside and out and allow to dry, before applying a third layer. When the box is completely dry, which may take some time, because the inner card will have absorbed some moisture, apply a primer. Gently rub down the surface with fine sandpaper when the primer is dry and retouch with primer if necessary. Decorate the surface with paint or with patterns cut from wall paper or from magazines (see Découpage for other suggestions). Apply a coat of varnish or clear polyurethane, leave to dry, rub down gently and apply a second coat of varnish or clear polyurethane. For a really hard, shiny finish, you may want to apply several coats of varnish. You must always make sure that the varnish is absolutely dry before you attempt to rub it down.

Papier mâché can also be used with a former that is removed when the layers of pasted paper are dry. Make a fruit bowl, for example, by taking two smooth-sided bowls, one larger than the other. Place the small bowl upside down on your work surface and balance the larger bowl on top. Check the proportions. The smaller bowl is going to be the foot of the bowl and it should not be too large. On the other hand, it should not be so small that the larger bowl looks as if it will topple over. When you are satisfied that the finished piece will look correctly proportioned, lightly grease the outside of each bowl. Apply several layers of pasted paper strips to the bowls, making sure that subsequent layers do not run in the same direction as the underlying layer. Neaten the top edges and allow to dry. You will probably find that the inner layers will not be able to dry out completely until you have removed the bowls. At this stage you can simply glue the two bowls together before painting and varnishing. However, you will obtain a neater edge if you glue lengths of cotton cord (the kind used to edge cushions is ideal) around the edge of the foot, around the joint between the two and, if you wish, around the top edge to create a neat lip. Cover the cord with a couple of layers of paper strips. Leave to dry before decorating and varnishing.

Paper pulp is usually used to shape decorations that are applied to objects made with pasted strips, and before you dismiss the idea out of hand, remember that in the last century pressed papier mâché was used to make very pretty and carefully modelled dolls' heads. Use the pulp with discretion to make some original and appropriate decorations for your fruit bowl. If you do not think that your artistic skills are sufficient for you to model fruits and flowers, press the pulp into the little plastic molds that are sold for molding chocolate or marzipan to create a pattern of flowers and leaves, or use real shells for a seaside theme. Allow them to dry partially before removing them from the molds and pasting them in position.

Candles

The heavenly aroma of real beeswax candles is immediately evocative of mellow flames, flickering softly on polished furniture. This is, of course, a false memory, for real beeswax has always been far too expensive for the production of candles for everyday use and was used only for church candles and for the homes of the rich. Until the mid-nineteenth century most candles were made of tallow, rendered down animal fat, which resembles suet. Not only did these candles produce a lot of smoke as they burned but they also had a most unpleasant smell. The discovery of stearin, which occurs naturally in many animal and vegetable fats, and paraffin wax, which is a by-product of petrol, changed all that, and today candles that burn steadily with little or no smoke and that are available in the most alluring range of colors, shapes and sizes can be bought almost everywhere. They can also be made at home with only a very few pieces of special equipment.

Candles have always played a major part in religious rituals. The Romans used to light candles to frighten away evil demons, and they are thought to have been used in Druid ceremonies. In the Christian church they are especially associated with Easter and Christmas, and during the eight days of the Jewish Hanukkah a candle is lit on each day of the festival. Candlemas, which is celebrated on 2 February and is a quarter day in Scotland, used to be known as the Feast of the Purification of the Virgin Mary (now the Presentation of the Lord), and in Roman Catholic churches the candles that will be needed throughout the year are blessed on that day. The Christian Candlemas is thought to be based on the Roman feast, the Lupercalia, which was held in mid-February to worship the god Faunus and which was a fertility rite.

Candles, therefore, are used to signify the renewal of life and of faith, but whatever their underlying totemic significance, there can be no doubt that today they usually have a more decorative function. Use tall, elegantly tapering candles, tinted to match your table linen, to grace a smart dinner table, or make bright, chunky candles for a barbecue. If you have a garden pool, use small, floating candles to add a touch of mystery to your summer dinner parties. You can buy special fragrances that are mixed, in tiny quantities, with the melted paraffin wax, so your candles can be used to add aroma as well as visual interest. It is even worth experimenting with the essences that are used by aromatherapists, but do be careful, because some of these react badly to heat, and instead of filling your sitting room with a delicious fragrance they will smoke and spit and give off an unpleasantly acrid smell. If you are planning to entertain outdoors, consider adding an anti-midge preparation to your candles to protect your guests from unwelcome bites and stings.

The basic materials for making candles are available in most craft shops. You need paraffin wax, stearin, wicking, candle dye and a mold. Stearin, which has a higher melting point than paraffin wax, is added so that candles do not bend and collapse as they burn down. It also makes white candles whiter and intensifies the color of dyed candles. You can buy paraffin wax already mixed with stearin, but in general you need have a mixture of paraffin wax and stearin that contains about 10 per cent stearin. In addition, you will need a source of heat, a double saucepan or bain-marie, a sugar ther-

Opposite: Remember to protect the surface beneath dipped candles with newspaper and to support the candles between dips so that they do not touch each other. The candles can be as fat or as thin as you wish. Dip the finished candles in clear, hot wax, trim the wicks and neaten the bases with a hot knife.

mometer, mold sealant (plasticine or softened adhesive "tak" will do the job), wicking needles, scissors, spoons, old jugs and lots of newspaper, which you should spread liberally over both your working surface and the floor around you.

You will find a variety of ready-made molds in your local craft shop. Some of these are of rigid plastic – stars, spheres, cylinders and all manner of geometric shapes – and some are flexible rubber. These flexible molds are ideal for candles with textured patterns or for unusual shapes. You can, for example, create an entire fruit bowl, including grapes and bananas, from molded candles. Before you buy special molds, however, look around your home. You are almost certain to find containers that can be pressed into service as improvised molds. All you need bear in mind is that the container must be made of a material that will not melt, distort or shatter when the hot wax is poured in. You should also choose a shape from which the solid candle can be easily removed – that is, the shape should be wider at the top than at the base, unless, of course, you are prepared to break the container to remove the candle. Using a proprietary release agent on the inside of the mold will make it even easier to turn out the finished candle. Small terra-cotta or clay plant pots are ideal containers for candles for outdoors, and you do not even have to turn them out before use.

Having found a suitable mold, prepare the wick. This is plaited cotton, impregnated with chemicals so that it delivers the flame to the vapors in the wax. It is sold in a range of thicknesses to be used according to the diameter of the candle and is conveniently so labelled: a candle 3in (7.5cm) in diameter needs 3in (7.5cm) wicking – what could be simpler? Shop-bought molds will have a hole through which the wick can be inserted before the melted wax is poured in. This is where you need to use a mold sealant. The other end of the wick is supported on a skewer or length of dowel that rests on the top of the mold so that the wick is held taut, vertically and centrally, in the mold. If your mold does not already have a hole in the base through which the wick can be threaded or if you cannot make a suitable hole, prepare lengths of wicking by dipping them in clear molten wax and straightening them carefully. When the wicking is stiff, it can be inserted into a hole made in the finished candle with a hot wicking needle or fine, metal knitting needle.

When you have prepared the mold and the wick, heat the wax. Because paraffin wax is available in such a range of qualities, the melting point will vary depending on where and when you bought it. In general, however, you need to heat it to about 195°F (90°C), and you must use a double saucepan. Do not be tempted to melt wax over direct heat. Because water cannot get hotter than 212°F (100°C), the melting wax in the top saucepan will not overheat. Use a sugar thermometer to check the temperature of the melted wax from time to time, and to ensure that if you have to reheat it you achieve the same temperature.

Take sensible precautions while you are heating the wax. Make sure that the handles of the bain-marie or of your saucepans do not overhang the edge of your oven. Do not leave the wax unattended while it is melting. If it does catch light, turn off the source of heat and smother the flames with the lid of the saucepan or a dampened towel. Never, ever pour water on the flames. Do not try to move the saucepan. If hot wax splashes on your skin, hold the affected area under cold running water, which will immediately solidify the wax, then treat as you would for an ordinary burn or scald.

Add flakes of candle dye while the wax is melting. These discs are extremely concentrated and you need only use a very small amount. Begin with a single color – a brilliant red star-shaped candle would be a wonderful centrepiece for a Christmas dinner table. Alternatively, allow the wax to cool a little before you add the dye and then stir it in lightly so that you achieve a marbled effect. Candle dyes have the advantage that they can be mixed with each other to create a vast range of tones and colors, and some of the most effective candles are those that are a subtle gradation of shades of a single color. When you are mixing the dyes, remember that while the tone can be darkened it cannot be lightened. Striped candles made in tones of a single color need, ideally, to be made upside down, so that, when the candle is turned out of the mold, the darkest shade is at the base.

If you want to make striped candles, add the first batch of wax and wait until it has begun to set before adding the next. If the first layer of wax is allowed to set too much, the second layer will not adhere to it properly. If it is not sufficiently set, the two layers will bubble together and you will have an uneven, possibly unattractive area (although this may be an effect that you want to achieve, so it is worth experimenting). Clear plastic molds make it easy to judge the depth of the different layers, and they are, for that reason alone, perhaps easier to use for your first few attempts. Candles with angled stripes can be made simply by supporting the mold at an angle while the various layers set. For an even more sophisticated effect, turn the supported mold through 90 degrees before you add the next layer. Make sure that you pour the molten wax into the centre of the mold and avoid getting splashes on the sides, which will spoil the appearance of the finished candle.

When the candle is quite set, remove it from the mold. If the surface is not as regular as you would like, use a hot knife to smooth it. If it is badly pitted, make a virtue of necessity and use the round end of a small ball-peen hammer to indent a regular pattern over the surface. Then dip the candle into a bath of hot paraffin wax (with no added stearin) to give it a glossy finish. If a cylindrical candle is not as perfectly cylindrical as you had hoped, use a hot, sharp knife to make it octagonal. And if it is a complete disaster, melt it down and begin again.

It is, of course, possible to buy real beeswax, and for a special occasion the extra expense will be amply rewarded. Adding small amounts of beeswax to paraffin wax will both improve the quality of the flame and impart a deliciously subtle aroma. You will, however, also find beeswax in the form of sheets, which can be simply rolled around a length of wicking to make elegant candles that burn with a steady flame and exude that delightful, evocative fragrance. Vary the form by using scissors or a craft knife to cut the rectangles of wax in half diagonally, then roll them carefully around the wick, which is laid along the short, upright edge of the triangle, to create two neatly tapering candles. If you are really thoughtful, you will roll the triangles of wax in opposite directions so that you have two perfect mirror-image candles.

The traditional way of making candles and also one of the simplest methods is by dipping lengths of prepared wick into deep containers of colored wax. This technique produces tall, smooth candles for a sophisticated dinner table. You will need a deep jug in which to melt the paraffin wax and you will also need some arrangement of hooks so that you can hang up the candles while they set. These candles are traditionally made in pairs, but you might want to begin by making just one until you are familiar with the method.

1. Melt the paraffin wax, stearin and dye in your container. If you are using a single length of wicking (the narrowest you can find), tie one end securely round a length of dowel or something similar. If you are making two candles, you will need a double length of wicking. The finished candles will be about 12in (30cm) high, so allow about 15in (38cm) of wicking for each.

2. Dip the wicking in the melted wax and remove it. Carefully pull it straight while it is still pliable and wait for a minute or two.

3. Continue to dip the coated wicking in the molten wax. After each dipping, allow the wax to harden, supporting the wick on hooks.

Candle dyes are available in a wide range of colors. You need add only a few flakes from a disc of dye to the molten wax to create a rainbow of shades. Dipped candles, such as those shown here, are traditionally made in pairs, with both ends of a long piece of wicking dipped into the wax.

These pretty napkin rings were made with plaits of salt dough, and decorated with brightly colored flowers made from tiny pieces of left-over dough. Remember to varnish the inside of the rings as well as the outside so that the dough is protected from damp air.

Salt Dough

It is scarcely possible to walk into a bookshop without finding at least one title, more probably half a dozen, on making and using salt dough. Most of these include instructions on making appealing or, depending on your view, twee little figures, brightly colored with vegetable cooking dyes. Once made, the little figures stand around on your windowsills, gathering dust, until, because they have been imperfectly varnished, they begin to crumble away.

Salt dough can have a place in the country kitchen, however, and not just as a pleasant and harmless way of occupying children on a wet afternoon. Put all thoughts of pink teddy bears and blue rabbits out of your mind and think instead of golden-brown sheaves of wheat or a subtly shaped and colored wreath or, more practically, a lattice basket to hold bread rolls on the breakfast table.

The ingredients for salt dough are perfectly simple: two parts of plain flour, to one part salt, a small amount of cooking oil and water to mix. Use ordinary table salt rather than sea salt because not only will the crystals of sea salt be visible in the finished dough but the salt can hurt your hands as you knead the dough. Mix the ingredients together to form a smooth, firm paste. Try to avoid over mixing – you do not want to trap air in the mixture because it will create unattractive bubbles in the finished piece.

132

Form the plaits for the napkin rings into neat circles around a narrow jar or bottle, which should be lightly greased so that it can be easily removed without distorting the shape of the ring.

Some recipes omit the oil; other recipes suggest the addition of a small amount of wallpaper paste. Including oil does make for a smoother dough, but it is really a matter of preference. If you wish, add one or two drops of vegetable food colorants at this stage, kneading the dye thoroughly through the dough. More natural shades can be achieved by adding instant coffee.

When you have prepared the dough, roll it out carefully on a lightly floured board. Use biscuit and pastry cutters and cut out shapes, or press small amounts of dough into the small molds you can buy in good cook ware shops for making chocolate and marzipan shapes. It is probably easiest to make flat objects directly on a lightly greased backing sheet, so that carefully shaped and decorated pieces do not become misshapen or damaged as you try to move them. If you wish, lightly glaze with beaten egg white, which can also be used to make individual shapes adhere to each other.

If you want to make a lattice bowl, use an appropriately shaped oven-proof mixing bowl as a former and stand it upside down on a baking tray. Carefully cover the bowl with kitchen foil, smoothing out as many creases as you can and turning the foil under the edge of bowl. Then carefully arrange the dough strips over the base of the bowl, overlapping them to create a woven affect. Add a plait or twist of dough around the edge to finish it off neatly. Place the bowl in the oven and half cook it. As soon as the dough is firm enough to hold its shape, remove the bowl and foil and return the dough to the oven to finish baking.

There are almost as many recommended cooking times for salt dough as there are recipes for mixing it. Ideally, the more delicate the piece, the lower the temperature – try setting your oven at 250°F/120°C/gas mark 1–2 and leaving the dough in for between 1½ and 2 hours. Small objects, of course, require a fraction of that time. Make sure that the surface does not burn, protecting it with a piece of baking parchment if necessary. When the dough is cooked it should be a delicate golden color and it will feel crisp and dry. If you are going to paint or varnish the dough, it must be bone dry. The slightest dampness will prevent the paint from adhering to the surface and the dough will eventually rot and crumble away. Carefully apply a coat of spirit-based varnish, which will help to protect the finished piece from moisture in the atmosphere.

You are almost certain to have the ingredients for salt dough already to hand in your kitchen. Use a recipe that suits you, but do not overwork the dough or it will crack and crumble as it cooks.

Project
Dough Wreath

This little wreath would be a pretty decoration on a kitchen wall, but remember not to hang it where it is likely to be subject to steam or sudden changes in temperature. Make a hanger from an ordinary paper clip, cut in half with pliers, and insert it before baking. If you forget about the hanger, wait until you have baked the dough and it is completely cold, then use strong glue to attach an ordinary picture hook.

1. Prepare the dough and divide it into three equal amounts. Cover one portion with kitchen film while you roll the other two pieces into long, smooth rolls. Twist the two rolls together on your work surface to make a neat, regular twist.

2. Place a jam jar or something similar on a lightly greased baking tray and arrange the twist around the jam jar. Trim the ends and use a little water to hold the ends together. Remove the jar. Roll out the remaining portion of dough and use a sharp knife and ruler to cut strips to make a bow, which should be positioned over the join in the circle of dough. Brush with beaten egg white before baking or varnish after baking.

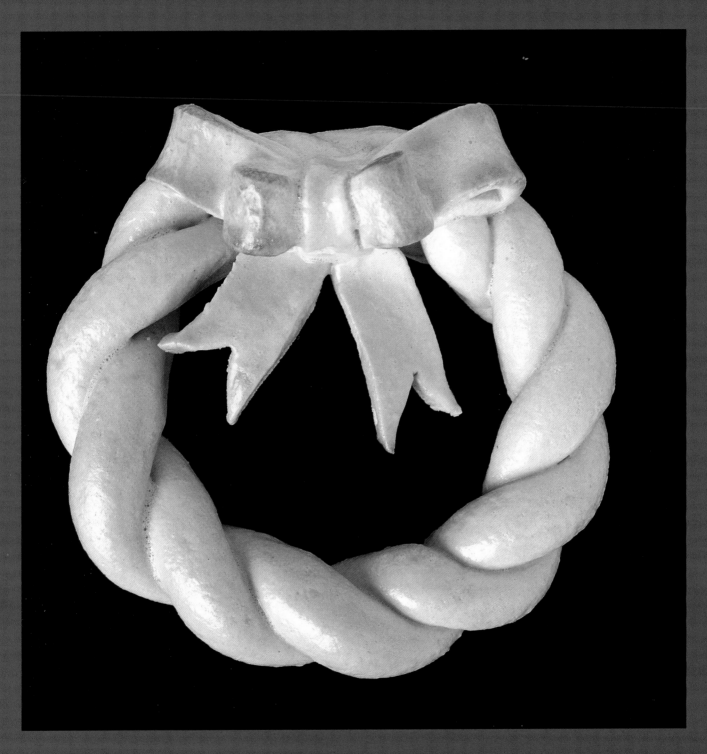

3. We left the wreath plain, but if you wish you could color the bow. The charm of the plain dough lies in the delicate color to which parts of it turn as it bakes.

Project
Dough Basket

Salt dough, glazed with beaten egg white, is the ideal medium for making this useful little basket for bread rolls. Shaping the base is the most difficult part.

1. Divide the dough into two and cover one portion with cling film so that it does not dry out. Roll out the other piece until it is fairly thin, shaping it into a long rectangle. Use a ruler and sharp knife to cut strips that are about ¹/₂in (1cm) wide.

2. Arrange the strips on a sheet of kitchen film over a baking tray or board, weaving them over and under each other to create the basket-like appearance. Place a lightly greased ovenproof bowl in the centre of the woven pieces. Turn the bowl, dough, film and tray upside down and take away the tray and the film. If you are lucky, the woven strips will be left, draped smoothly over the base of the bowl. Trim the ends of the strips and bend them out slightly before baking, still draped over the inverted bowl.

3. Meantime, use the remaining dough to make two long, thin rolls. Twine them together to create a circle that will fit on top of the woven base. Use the trimmings of dough to shape some ears of corn and use them to decorate the circular twist and to disguise the join. Brush with beaten egg white and bake. When both sections are completely dry and cool, use strong adhesive to join them together.

GLOSSARY

Acrylic paint Artists' acrylic paints, supplied in tubes, are water based and can, therefore, be mixed with water as well as with each other. When dry, they are waterproof and must be removed with methylated spirits (denatured alcohol). Widely available, there is a huge range of colours.

Appliqué The name given to the technique of placing pieces of fabric on other fabrics to create geometric or pictorial designs.

Awl A tool used in basket making to open spaces between weaving or to tuck in ends.

Bargello Also known as Florentine stitch, a type of needlepoint in which series of upright stitches are worked to create repeating, usually geometric, patterns.

Beading In basket making a round cane that runs around the edge and hides the threading holes.

Between A sewing needle similar to a sharp (*q.v.*) but shorter. Betweens are often used for quilting.

Bodkin (1) A screwdriver-like tool used in basket-making to open spaces in weaving. (2) A thick, blunt-ended needle, used for drawing tape, ribbon or elastic through hems and so forth.

Bolt The name of the bundles in which the rush for basket making is purchased.

Border In basket making the name given to the top edge.

Brake A short length of reed, woven alternately above the beginning of a weaver (*q.v.*) to hold it in position.

Canvas Available in two main kinds – single thread (mono) and double thread (Penelope). Single thread has a simple over and under weave and is suitable for most canvas work projects. It does tend to distort as it is stitched, and best results will be obtained with a frame. Interlock (*q.v.*), a kind of mono canvas, is more stable. Double thread canvas has pairs of threads, woven together, and it is a firm, stable material. Canvas is available in a range of sizes or gauges, known as mesh, which are identified by the number of holes to the inch – for example, 14-inch mesh has 14 holes to the inch. The most often used sizes are from 10- to 16 mesh. Rugs require a 5- or 7-mesh canvas.

Ceramic paint This can be either oil based or water based. Check before you buy, because some kinds need to be fired to set the paint.

Charting paper Tracing paper with printed graph lines is available in the same mesh sizes as evenweave fabrics (*q.v.*).

Coil A weaving technique in basket making that works from an inner core outwards, winding about itself.

Contact adhesive Available under several trade names, this adhesive bonds immediately, allowing no time to reposition pieces.

Crackle varnish Sometimes sold as cracklure, this is a two-stage varnish. Two separate coats are applied, and the first, slow-drying coat continues to dry under the second, quick-drying coat, creating cracks in the surface, which can be patinated with artists' oil paints to reveal the cracks. The results can be unpredictable. Always check the manufacturer's instructions before use.

Crewel needle The most useful embroidery needle, with a long eye and fine point. The eye will take several strands of thread.

Emulsion (latex) paint The most widely available paint, found in all do-it-yourself stores. The paint is water-based but is waterproof when dry. Use on porous surfaces for best results and look out for small, trial pots, which are economic for small-scale projects.

Epoxy resin Available under several trade names, this is a useful adhesive for china, glass and metal repairs. It is usually supplied in two parts – glue and hardener – and provides a strong join. It is too expensive for large-scale projects, however.

Evenweave fabric The most suitable material for cross stitch projects, evenweave fabrics have an equal number of weft and warp threads in a square area. Available in a range of colours, including pastel and deep-dyed, evenweave fabrics are available in a variety of counts (that is, holes to the inch) and several widths. Choose a fabric in which the holes are clearly visible.

Interlock mono canvas The vertical and horizontal threads are bonded at the intersections, rather than simply passing above and below each other as in regular canvas (*q.v.*). Do not use interlock canvas for items such as cushion covers because it is not flexible enough.

Isometric paper A type of graph paper marked in triangles, which is useful for preparing templates for patchwork schemes.

Medium density fiberboard (MDF) A comparatively lightweight, artificially made "wood". Treat it as you would ordinary wood.

Oil paint Artists' oil paints, supplied in tubes, are oil based and can be dissolved with turpentine or white (mineral) spirit. Suitable for almost any surface.

Pearl cotton Also known as coton perlé, this twisted thread has a slight sheen. It is available in a range of thicknesses, the finest designated by the highest numbers.

PVA adhesive (polyvinyl acetate) One of the most useful adhesives for craft use. It can be thinned with water or used straight from the tin. Use a thinned solution as a primer for porous surfaces.

Rattan cane A material used in seating, usually supplied in bundles. Sometimes also known as glossy or chair-seating cane.

Rush The stem of marsh or waterside plants that is used to making chair seats. Lengths of rush, sold in bolts, can be plaited for strength.

Sharp A sewing needle with a small eye for general sewing.

Stake The sections of the woven base in basket making that are bent upwards to create the vertical elements through which the lengths of rush and so forth are woven.

Stranded cottons There is a huge range of colours from the major manufacturers. Check the manufacturer and number when buying to ensure a good match and avoid mixing cottons from different manufacturers in the same project.

Tapestry needle A blunt-ended needle with a large eye, which is suitable for inserting between threads without piercing them. Use a tapestry needle for needlepoint and counted thread work.

Trapunto A type of quilting in which selected areas of a pattern or design are padded. The patterns are defined by lines of backstitch or running stitch.

Weaver In basket making the working length of rush, cane and so on, woven in and out of the stakes (*q.v.*) to create the base and sides of the object.

Wholecloth quilt Traditionally stitched with a thread that matches the colour of the fabric.

INDEX

PICTURE
CREDITS

Marshall Cavendish Picture Library: 8, 9, 10, 11, 15, 21, 22, 25, 27, 29, 30/31, 32, 34, 35, 36, 37 (top), 40, 41 (top), 44, 45, 46, 47, 48, 52, 53, 54, 59, 61 (bottom), 65, 66. 67, 69, 70, 71, 72, 73, 76, 84, 85, 86, 97, 101, 102, 103, 115, 116, 117, 121, 122, 123, 124, 130, 131, 132, 133, 134/135, 136, 137, 138, 139.

Ingrid Mason Picture Library: IMP/Marie-Louise Avery: 18, 24, 37, 42, 90/91, 106, 110; IMP/William Mason: 56,57, 58, 104, 105, 107.

New England Stock Photo: NESP/Margo Tuissig Pinkerton: 11, 83; NESP/Leslie O'Shaughnessy: 16/17, 38, 39.

Picture Perfect USA: 6/7, 12/13, 50/51, 80/81, 92/93, 98/99, 118/119.

Reed International Books: RIB/Bill McLaughlin: 74, 87 (bottom); RIB/Rob Matheson: 87 (top).

Shelly Zegart: 60, 61, 62, 63, 64, 75.